D1081652

In the
Bunker
with Hitler

In the
Bunker
with Hitler

23 JULY 1944 – 29 APRIL 1945

Bernd Freytag von Loringhoven

PEGASUS BOOKS
NEW YORK

IN THE BUNKER WITH HITLER

Pegasus Books LLC
45 Wall Street, Suite 1021
New York, NY 10005

Copyright © 2005 by Editions Perrin

Original edition Dans le bunker de Hitler published by
Editions Perrin, Paris, 2005

First published in English in 2006 by
The Orion Publishing Group

English translation copyright © 2006 by John Gilbert

First Pegasus Books edition 2007

Library of Congress Cataloging-in-Publication Data is available.

ISBN: 978-1-933648-39-2

Printed in the United States of America
Distributed by Consortium

Contents

List of Photographs and Maps

Hermann Göring 108

Albert Speer and Adolf Hitler 133

Paul Joseph and Magda Goebbels 151

Eva Braun 161

Joachim von Ribbentrop 165

Karl Dönitz 172

PLATE SECTION (BETWEEN PAGES 96–97)

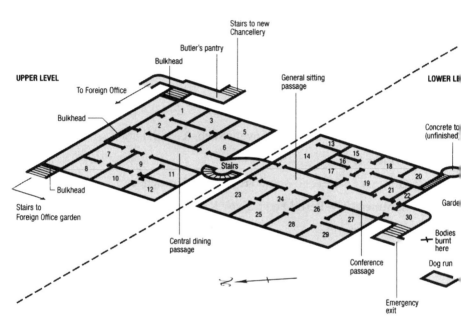

UPPER LEVEL

Stairs to new Chancellery

Butler's pantry

Bulkhead

To Foreign Office

Bulkhead

Stairs to
Foreign Office garden

Bulkhead

General sitting passage

LOWER LE

Concrete to
(unfinished

Stairs

Garde

Central dining passage

Conference passage

Bodies
burnt
here

Dog run

Emergency exit

1–4	Kitchens, etc.	20	Hitler's bedroom
5–6	Lumber rooms	21	'Map room' or conference room
7–8	Servants' quarters	22	'Dog-bunker' or guards' room
9–12	Frau Goebbels' and children's rooms	23	Power house (diesel engine)
13	Electric light switchboard	24	Telephone and guard room
14	WCs	25	Emergency telephone exchange
15	Private bathroom	26	Drawing room
16	Eva Braun's dressing room	27	Goebbels' bedroom (previously Morell's)
17	Eva Braun's bed-sitting room	28–29	Stumpfegger's room
18	Hitler's study	30	Anteroom and cloakroom
19	Anteroom to Hitler's suite		

Plan of Hitler's Bunker

Foreword

Sixty years ago one of the most terrible wars in history came to an end. It was a shattering experience for those caught up in it, and it is seared upon the memory of those of us who survived. In the dead of night, images of bloody combat still haunt me, and I see visions of friends who died far from their homes and families. Many of their graves have since disappeared, but the unfading recollection of these comrades remains alive.

Death was a constant companion on the battlefront, and never more so than in Russia. But more than death itself, our greatest fear was to be taken prisoner by the enemy. Captivity within the Soviet Union inevitably entailed, in our imaginations, suffering in its most terrible forms; cold, hunger, inhuman treatment, sickness and, ultimately, a miserable end.

On three occasions, with God's help, I narrowly avoided such a fate. In January 1943, three days before the last German aeroplane landed at Gumrak airport, I escaped from the Stalingrad pocket. Out of 90,000 German soldiers of the Sixth Army, only 5,000 survived captivity. In late summer of that same year, thanks to a German reconnaissance aircraft, I helped prevent the last remnants of German troops on the Mius front from being wiped out by Soviet forces. And on 29 April 1945 I managed to get away from Berlin, then encircled by the Red Army, after an eventful journey through the Russian lines as their troops struck out towards the west.

FOR A PERIOD of some nine months, from 23 July 1944 to 29 April 1945, I had the opportunity – extremely rare for a young officer such as myself – of being with Hitler almost every day. In my capacity as aide-de-camp, I attended, with the Army chief of staff, General Heinz Guderian, and subsequently his successor, General Hans Krebs, the daily situation conferences presided over by the Führer. These meetings brought together the highest-ranking representatives of the military hierarchy, such as Marshals Keitel and Göring, General Jodl, Admiral Dönitz, and several of the top men of the Nazi regime, notably Himmler, Goebbels, Bormann and Ribbentrop. By then Hitler spent most of his time presiding over the Führerlage, the daily meeting where he exercised his authority as head of the armed forces and where he continued to make operational decisions on every front. I was personally present at these highly confidential discussions.

AFTER I WAS FREED from prisoner-of-war camp early in 1948, I began to write about my experiences of that hideous yet fascinating period, still fresh in my memory. I had kept four longhand 'wartime logs' – notebooks made up of sheets of white paper distributed in the camp by the American YMCA (Young Men's Christian Association). Now, almost sixty years later, these notes have served as the basis of the present book.

During my captivity, I never concealed from my British inter-rogators any of my activities in the final months of the war, nor my participation in top-level military meetings. I had not committed any actions contrary to international law, nor had I done anything for which I felt personally culpable. At the same time, however, I had continued to do my duty as a soldier at the behest of a criminal. It was hard to make my British questioners understand the ambivalence of my situation. Deep down, I was hostile to Hitler, yet I had wished to serve my country. In this book I try to show how a young officer, duti-fully loyal to the end, could nevertheless remain faithful to his inherent beliefs and values.

I MUST THANK François and Monica d'Alançon for having suggested and encouraged me to write this book. Our lengthy meetings through the summer of 2004 were the catalyst to its becoming a reality. Two and a half years in British captivity were a hard time, but they could not be compared with an equivalent in a Soviet prison camp. Although I was sometimes very angry with the way I was treated by the British soldiers, I never lost my respect for the British nation and my sympathy for the British way of life.

After the war – in the Bundeswehr – I got in touch with many British officers and I regarded it as a great fortune that I made friends with them. I might mention my dear fellow Brigade Commander Major-General Philip Tower, later Commandant of the Royal Military Academy at Sandhurst, and especially General Sir John Hackett, who commanded the British Army in Germany in the sixties. When we had both retired from active service Sir John was pleased to see my son Arndt accepted at New College, University of Oxford, where Sir John was an Honorary Fellow. My son studied four years in Oxford and left as an M.A. I was grateful that my son had the opportunity to study in one of the best universities in the world, and that he was deeply influenced by its free, liberal and democratic spirit for his own lifetime.

ONE

My first meeting with Hitler

I shall never forget the day when I first met Hitler face to face: it was 23 July 1944, in East Prussia. Three days following the failure of the attempt on his life in the July Plot, and the day after I took up the post of his aide-de-camp, I accompanied General Heinz Guderian to the Führer's headquarters, some twenty kilometres from the Army HQ near Rastenburg. Access to the so-called *Wolfsschanze* (Wolf's Lair) was closed to all strangers. During this summer of 1944, work was still going on to transform the place into a veritable fortress.

Our car passed the outer security perimeter in the shape of a manned checkpoint, reinforced by barbed wire and the notice 'Beware – Mines!' on either side of the road. After an identity check we entered the forbidden zone before being confronted by further roadblocks. After several more checks – carried out this time by the Waffen-SS – we were waved through into the Führer's inner sanctum. The security force deployed here, not counting

Hitler's own bodyguards, was the size of a brigade, fully mechanised and equipped with the latest weapons. Anti-aircraft batteries protected the entire installation. The Führer himself lived in an enormous bunker with a ceiling no less than eight metres thick. The construction of all Hitler's bunker complexes was dictated by the bombing capabilities of the Allied air forces. As soon as a more powerful bomb was identified within the enemy arsenal, the ceilings of the bunkers variously assigned as the Führer's headquarters were strengthened accordingly.

SS guards conducted us to a room reserved for situation conferences – a wooden hut similar to the one where the attack on the Führer had taken place. Before being allowed in, each of us had to surrender his weapon. Since the day of the attack, everyone, excepting only generals, had been systematically searched. As a young officer, I was unused to this and found the procedure humiliating. On that day some twenty people were standing around awaiting the Führer's arrival, chatting. In the centre of the room there was an enormous table, on which maps were spread out. I had already caught a glimpse of the debris lying around in the adjacent hut, bits of beams and planks blackened by the explosion of the bomb placed there by Colonel Claus Schenk Graf von Stauffenberg. Now, three days later, Hitler's colleagues still bore traces of the blast. Field Marshal Keitel and others had cotton wool stuffed in their ears to protect their damaged eardrums. General Jodl had a turban-like bandage round his head. One officer present had his arm in a sling, others had facial burn marks.

I HAVE NEVER forgotten the impression that Hitler made on me as he entered the room. I had seen the Führer once before, in the spring of 1939, at a big military march-past put on for the visit of the Prince-Regent of Yugoslavia. My regiment had taken part in it and I happened to be only thirty metres or so from the reviewing platform. You did not have to be a Nazi to be struck by his powerful, dynamic presence. That was the image of him I retained, reinforced by subsequent newsreels and newspapers. Now, on 23 July 1944, the man who stood before me was nothing like that. This was no 'Reichsführer of Greater Germany fighting for his destiny'. At fifty-five years old, he truly looked an old man, stooping, hunched, head drooping, skin greyish, face deathly pale, eyes lacklustre. He shuffled forward, dragging his left leg, the right arm, slightly injured by the explosion, held stiffly. Guderian introduced me. With a weary smile, Hitler gave me a limp handshake, murmuring a few words of welcome. I was taken aghast. The hero lauded by official propaganda was a wreck. How could this be? Over the coming months I began to understand. It was like looking at a waxwork. For a fleeting moment the thought crossed my mind: this man with the appearance and demeanour of a tramp is none the less sole ruler of the Reich!

TWO

The Army: a last resort

I come from an ancient family, originally from Westphalia, but which settled in the Baltic region in the fifteenth century. Previously, the Order of Teutonic Knights, ejected from the Holy Land by the Arabs, had sought new homes in Latvia and Estonia. Johann Freytag von Loringhoven, master of the Order in Livonia from 1484 to 1493, had left his estate to his nephew Arndt who, newly arrived from Westphalia, was the founder of our family. So our links with Russia, which had controlled the Baltic provinces since the conquest by Peter the Great at the start of the eighteenth century, went back a long way. One of my ancestors, Karl Johann, had been a colonel in the guard of Tsar Alexander I during the Napoleonic Wars. In 1814 he moved to France, having married Charlotte Benoit d'Anrosey, daughter of the owner of the chateau of Avize, in Champagne, in what you might term a small gesture of Franco-Russian reconciliation. On the day that his wife inherited the property, they had left St Petersburg to live there. Later, as a widower, he continued to live on the estate for another twenty years. When the chateau was finally sold in 1848, the tsar authorised him to import into Russia, without any customs duty, 10,000 bottles of champagne. The last bottle was drunk at the christening of my father in 1879.

On my mother's side, the family, who came from Thuringia, had settled in Estonia in 1390. Otto Berend von Moller, one of my maternal ancestors, had been Minister of the Navy to Tsar Nicholas I.

I was born in 1914, just before the First World War, at Arensburg, on the island of Ösel in Estonia, today known as Saaremaa, where my family owned a property of 1,500 hectares. My grandfather was still running the place when we were dispossessed in 1919. My father, like all Germans of military age in the Baltic provinces, fought against the Bolsheviks on the Narva front, in eastern Estonia, until 1920. When German soldiers seized control of the island and drove out the Russians in October 1917, several officers were billeted with my parents. Among them was Eduard Arnhold, a reserve lieutenant and a banker from Berlin, who was a Jew. My parents treated him like the other German officers, and made friends with him. When we arrived in Germany as refugees, the Arnholds generously helped my mother by inviting her to Berlin. In 1937 I stayed with these Jewish friends of ours in their Berlin apartment. With the anti-Semitic political climate deteriorating daily, their belongings were under threat of confiscation, and they were gravely concerned for their future. Later that year, the Arnholds succeeded in emigrating to California. After the war they resumed communications with my mother and sent her CARE parcels. At her request, when I was in a British POW camp in Ostend, they sent me a German–English dictionary, sorely needed as I had started to work as an interpreter.

In the spring of 1919, as conditions became more dangerous, my mother and her parents left Estonia to find refuge in Misdroy, a seaside resort in Pomerania. My parents were soon separated by post-war events and I was educated by my mother and my grandparents. My father, having graduated in law from St Petersburg University, and speaking several languages, meanwhile resumed his studies after reaching Germany, and obtained a doctorate in chemistry at Greifswald University in Pomerania. The economic crisis of 1929 forced him out of his job in a tyre factory at Fulda (Hesse) and he ended his professional life as administrator of the Lutheran Church in Mecklenburg.

IN SPITE OF financial difficulties, I enjoyed a happy childhood. I was sent to the Baltenschule at Misdroy, a school founded by teachers who, like us, were refugees from the Baltic region; here I made many friends. We were educated in a spirit that struck a balance between conservatism and liberalism. My father, a devout Protestant, was disturbed at the Nazis' hostility to religion, whereas my mother was completely uninterested in politics. Given that we were Germans of Baltic origin, we were violently opposed to Communism as a result of our experience with the Bolsheviks in 1918–19; and the rumours of the terrible treatment meted out to the middle classes and aristocracy in Russia merely strengthened our feeling. German middle-class political parties shared this anti-Communist sentiment, which was by no means confined to the National Socialist Party (NDSAP). Yet at the same time we had for years been on familiar terms with Russians at first-hand. Until the final days of the empire, Germans living in the Baltic provinces maintained close links with Russia, and had played a major role both in its government and armed forces.

Like many others, my family was deeply critical of the inefficiency of the Weimar Republic. The German people were having a taste of parliamentary democracy, but the constitution had shortcomings. The disintegration of parliament into a multitude of political parties made it extremely difficult to form a government majority. Germany had some six million unemployed. Many – and not only on the right – longed for law and order, and an improvement in the economy. In that context, Hitler came across as an extremely dynamic individual, but nevertheless 'working class'. We were wary and distrustful because we could not fathom his true objectives. My uncle Axel, professor of international law at Breslau, had been elected Reichstag deputy for the Deutschnationale Volkspartei (DNVP), but I was unable to reconcile myself to the ultra-conservative, anti-Semitic views of that nationalist, monarchical party. I inclined more towards the politics of Gustav Stresemann, Minister of Foreign Affairs between 1923 and 1929, who supported a resumption of negotiations to mitigate the detrimental effects of the Versailles Treaty, to which end he had successful discussions with his French counterpart, Aristide Briand.

When I graduated in 1932, I never dreamed of pursuing a military career. I would have preferred to study history, but that was not exactly conducive to earning a living. So I decided to go in for law at the University of Königsberg in East Prussia, where my father's brother had settled. Professor Rothfels, an officer during the First World War, a Jew and a brilliant teacher, was offering a very popular course on Bismarck. When the Nazis threatened to dismiss him from the university, his students did all they could to prevent him leaving but, towards the end of 1934, he was sacked, and emigrated. After the war, he was one of the first to write about the conspiracy of 20 July 1944.

I quickly realised that in order to make my way in the legal profession I would have to become a member of the National Socialist Party. After an initial examination, every budding lawyer was obliged to attend a training course where he would be indoctrinated with party ideology. Unless he went along with this he was excluded from gaining the necessary diploma to become a practising lawyer, judge or civil servant. My parents had lost everything in the First World War and I could not afford to go it alone. There would be no alternative but to join the Party. Long, hard reflection, however, persuaded me that to adopt a military career would protect me from any kind of compromise with National Socialism. Under the Weimar Republic, officers and soldiers of the Reichswehr swore allegiance not to the president of the Republic but to the constitution; they had no voting rights, they were not eligible for parliament and they were forbidden to belong to any political organisation. The Army stood quite aloof from party politics.

Another event helped me to make up my mind more quickly. On 30 June 1934, Hitler's 'night of the long knives' enabled him to get rid of Röhm, founder and organiser of the *Sturm-abteilungen* (SA), but in addition and, in my opinion, more importantly, to dispose of two generals, Kurt von Schleicher, former Chancellor of the Reich, and Ferdinand von Bredow. I was terribly shocked to hear the radio announcement justifying these killings, committed with utter impunity. Murder was evidently equated with an act of justice.

On 1 November 1934, I joined the 7th Breslau Cavalry Regiment as a cadet. Wessel Freytag von Loringhoven, a cousin fifteen years older than myself, was a captain in the regiment and had helped me get in. Moreover, my uncle Axel, the Reichstag deputy, had connections and influence in Silesia. The initial six-month training period was in no sense a sinecure. Twelve of us slept in a room with bunk beds, lying on straw mattresses and pillows.

After the death of President Hindenburg, all soldiers had to take an oath of allegiance to Hitler personally. That would indeed change all the rules. The wording of the new oath stipulated the 'Führer and Reich Chancellor'; yet to be honest, my young officer colleagues and myself considered it a matter of little concern, unlike those old-timers who had served under the emperor. Given the regiment's conventional views, we wanted nothing to do with the Nazis, simply to keep them at arms' length, and we did not feel compromised by what seemed to us a mere formality.

THE 'SMALL REICHSWEHR' of 100,000 men which had been set up by the Weimar Republic in accordance with the Treaty of Versailles included a relatively large number of cavalry regiments. After the First World War the cavalry was increasingly regarded as out of date; and the natural progression from cavalry to tank regiment therefore appeared a matter of common sense. In 1935, three cavalry regiments were dissolved and converted into tank regiments. Among these was the 7th Cavalry Regiment, descended from the cuirassiers of the Grand Elector of Brandenburg in the mid seventeenth century; it was now transformed into the 2nd Tank Regiment and moved to Eisenach, in Thuringia. The fact that the three dissolved regiments embodied the oldest traditions of the Army could have been purely coincidental, or it might have been the outcome of political intent. The Nazis distrusted tradition and associated conservative values.

In the 2nd Tank Regiment we were extremely fortunate to have Colonel von Prittwitz as our first commander. This Silesian aristocrat, formerly with the 7th Cavalry Regiment, adroitly struck a fine balance between traditional values and modern demands, while maintaining the uniformity of the corps of senior and junior officers. After being promoted general and divisional commander, Prittwitz was killed in 1942 at Tobruk, during the North African campaign.

THREE

War on all fronts

War clouds were gathering yet Hitler spoke of nothing other than peace. In 1938 my regiment was put on alert. After a series of exercises and manoeuvres, the signing of the Munich Agreement on 30 September came as a relief. We reckoned that Hitler's game was to bring pressure on the Allies to make concessions, but that he was not ready to go to war. The Führer was bent on obtaining, by peaceful means, the annulment of the Versailles Treaty and a political arrangement that would lead to the recovery of some of the German provinces in Poland, or at least access to East Prussia and Danzig. The transformation of the Weimar Republic's Reichswehr into a modern, all-powerful Wehrmacht lay as yet far in the future. To take the risk of unleashing a war with insufficient weaponry seemed to us wholly irresponsible. So the attack on Poland, on 1 September 1939, filled us with little enthusiasm. On the contrary, we felt we had been tricked.

I took part in the Polish campaign as ordnance officer to Major Walter Wenck, the G3 (Third General Staff Officer), responsible for the operation of the division – a talented officer, later to become general of the Twelfth Army. It was my baptism of fire. I was somewhat nervous as I thought back to the horrors of the First World War; but we soon came to recognise our superiority to the poorly equipped Polish troops. Even so, one night I lost two of my closest comrades – an experience which, more than any other, brought home to me the harsh reality of war. Captain Werner von Köckritz had led our company. I admired his character and presence, and was fortunate to be his friend. Lieutenant Georg Baron von Meyerndorff had studied with me in those early days at the Baltenschule. We shared a common Baltic background and a number of happy youthful memories. The Polish campaign ended in outright victory, yet I felt as if I were in mourning. I believe it was the only time I wept during the entire war.

EARLY IN OCTOBER 1939 our division was relocated to the Rhineland. We were much relieved to see this initial campaign concluded so swiftly. German losses were relatively light; for our part, we had inflicted terrible destruction and suffering on the Poles. But we had not the faintest idea of the terror yet to be unleashed on the population by the SS, the police and the Nazi administration. The massacre of the Jews and the persecution of the Slavs – described as Untermenschen ('subhumans') – had begun. The regime was intent on transforming Poland into a colony. Members of the intelligentsia, the nobility, the church and the middle classes were arrested and arbitrarily murdered. Owners of property were expropriated. On 25 October 1939, in order to leave the field open to the SS and the police, who complained of the Army's 'lack of understanding', Hitler replaced the military government by a civil administration. General Johannes Blaskowitz, Army commander in Poland, immediately denounced, in his written reports, the crimes committed by the SS, the police and the administration. We young officers became aware of the general's protests from rumours that had spread to the Rhineland. As was to be expected, Hitler ignored the accusations and General Walther von Brauchitsch, the Army commander-in-chief, gave way to Himmler. From then on General Blaskowitz was effectively silenced, and the persecutions continued by order of the governor-general, Hans Franck.

After spending the winter of 1939–40 in the Rhineland, in preparation for the offensive against France, we were placed on the alert every other day and were getting fed up with it. I was working permanently alongside Major Wenck in the 1st Panzer Division, commanded by General Kirchner. On 9 May 1940, Wenck went on leave for a couple of days. Around 13.30 hours Kirchner was called to the telephone: 'Yellow dossier, 10 May, 5.30 hours' said the voice at the end of the line. I was standing near the general and noticed that he showed no reaction. Kirchner, who did not know the details of the invasion plan,

Bernd Freytag von Loringhoven

photograph: author

had not understood the message. 'It's going to start tomorrow morning,' I explained to him, before going off to warn Wenck to get back to the division as soon as possible.

We were far from happy that evening before the attack. We knew something about the First World War from the books of Ernst Jünger and Erich Maria Remarque, and were aware of the terrible human losses suffered in the battles of Verdun, the Somme and so many others. We expected the French Army to put up a strong resistance; so we were all the more surprised when in a few weeks we reached Amiens, Dunkerque and Belfort.

Before the campaign began, the troops received strict instructions not to mingle with the civilian population. Any unit or individual violating this order would be liable to severe punishment. After the easy victories in Poland and France, a sense of superiority, verging upon euphoria, ran through the ranks, a feeling that was soon to be dissipated as the war on the eastern front continued without an end in sight. I remained in France during the summer of 1940, at Beaugency, on the River Loire working on plans for Operation Sea Lion, the invasion of Britain, which was destined never to take place.

In September I returned to take up a staff post under General Heinz Guderian, commander-in-chief of the Second Panzer Army, as aide-de-camp to Lieutenant Colonel Bayerlein, head of the Third Bureau and future chief of staff to General Rommel. We spent the winter planning Operation Barbarossa, the code-name for the campaign against the Soviet Union. In spring 1941 we moved from the Warsaw area to the Brest-Litovsk sector, prior to the opening of the Russian offensive on 22 June.

I had read Caulaincourt's memoirs on Napoleon's campaign in Russia and was distinctly uneasy as to the way things might turn out. In my opinion, there was no reason to attack the Soviet Union. The agreements signed between the Reich and Stalin had been respected; deliveries of wheat, oil and minerals had been coming in regularly by rail. The opening of a second front seemed absurd at a time when Britain was refusing peace negotiations and the United States was on the verge of entering the war. We soon realised that the Wehrmacht high command had been completely deceived in its estimation of Soviet military capacity. After the Army purges carried out by Stalin and the wretched failings of the Finnish campaign, expert German opinion that the Red Army had been irredeemably weakened proved to be wholly mistaken.

ON 22 JUNE, at around 3.00 a.m., the attack opened in an inferno of artillery fire. I had left headquarters, a few hundred metres from the frontier near Brest-Litovsk, in order to get as close as possible to the action and to observe the start of the offensive. I was lying in the grass on the bank of the river Bug when a battery of nearby rocket-launchers let loose a deafening salvo. Our armies quickly advanced through Minsk and Smolensk in the direction of Moscow. Guderian had under his command a division of tanks of the Waffen-SS which was being held in reserve while a company of SS stood guard over our head-quarters. Between Brest-Litovsk and Minsk, the speed of the advance meant that HQ was constantly on the move. One day, I was on my way to a new position with the chief of staff of our army, Colonel von Liebenstein, a Swabian aristocrat. On our arrival we came across several SS men who had lined up ten Russian prisoners in order to shoot them. 'Are you quite mad?' shouted the normally calm Liebenstein, jumping from his car. 'These are prisoners of war!' 'But, colonel, they are *Untermenschen*,' one of the SS protested. The prisoners' lives were spared.

At the end of August, on the Führer's orders and against the advice of the Army high command, we changed direction to the south, towards the Ukraine, where we lost precious time. Hitler wanted to occupy the Ukraine in order to deprive the Soviets of raw materials, and the Crimea to protect oil supplies from Romania. General Halder, chief of the general staff, considered it more important to capture Moscow, the most important strategic objective with its industry and communication infrastructure.

By late October we had reached Tula, only a hundred or so kilometres south of Moscow. Guderian's Second Panzer Army was advancing eastward, forming a large, almost unbroken circle. Guderian wanted to fall back to a narrower front, easier to defend, the only solution for avoiding heavy losses, in face of the Soviet counter-attack which was imminent. When we began our attack to the south of the Russian capital, in

Heinz Guderian

photograph © Austrian Archive/Corbis

mid-November, it was already too late, as winter was by now upon us. During the autumn, rain and mud had slowed our progress; in December the temperature fell to minus 36 degrees C. We were neither prepared nor equipped for such climatic conditions. Rifles seized up, oil froze. We had to light fires under the tanks to get them to move. Hitler would brook no talk of retreat. On 19 December, he personally took over supreme command of the Army, after the forced resignation of General von Brauchitsch. The following day, he forbade Guderian to withdraw his army to safer positions, prior to dismissing him on the day after Christmas. This decision appeared to me wholly unjustified.

In the spring of 1942, I rejoined the 2nd Tank Regiment, stationed in the Ukraine, in a battalion commanded by Lieutenant Colonel Hyazinth Graf von Strachwitz. This large Silesian landowner was also a dedicated soldier, possessed of flair and intuition. I remember how we passed one night, towards the end of May, in 'hedgehog position' – like a hedgehog spreading out his spines to all sides – isolated among Soviet troops in an attempt to block their escape from encirclement. At dawn Strachwitz called me over, along with a captain and a sergeant, to assess the situation. In front of us there were kurgans (Mongolian tombs), located on hills ten metres or so above the level of the steppe. The captain climbed one of these, together with the sergeant, to look around through binoculars. We joined them and saw Russian soldiers trying to avoid being encircled. A

Russian battery was firing at another hill. Suddenly, Strachwitz grabbed my arm and dragged me down the slope. A grenade exploded at the very spot where we had been standing and killed the captain and his sergeant. Strachwitz immediately ordered all engines to be revved up. The tanks and accompanying vehicles charged en bloc through the Russian lines to rejoin the rest of our division. Strachwitz's incredible instinct had saved my life.

AT THIS TIME, having been promoted captain, I commanded the 2nd Company of the regiment. Our brand new Panzer III tanks, armed with 50mm guns, soon proved themselves inferior to the Soviet T-34s, with their reinforced armour plating, lower silhouette and more efficient 76.2mm guns. We could only open fire on the T-34 at a distance of 300 metres and then only against the side, where the armour plating was thinner than at the front. Throughout the summer of 1942 there had been continuous tank battles on the steppes of the Ukraine. Our prime objective was Kalach, on the Don. In that immense open steppe, flat and uninhabited, you felt as if you were at sea. Yet nowhere else had we enjoyed such freedom of movement.

One day, we were confronted by a veritable armada of Russian tanks, T-34s and the even more powerful Stalins. A frontal attack along the centre of the plain would have cost us heavy casualties, since the T-34s could open fire from a kilometre away. I had decided, therefore, to get round the enemy in a concealed arc. When my company reached a position behind the

Soviets, I launched the attack. The Russians were so surprised that they took flight. One Stalin tank remained in front of us, immobilised by engine failure. We opened fire with no less than 142 50mm shells, but the projectiles simply ricocheted off the tank without piercing its armour. All of a sudden the turret moved slightly. I gave my company orders over the radio to cease fire. After the deafening din, everything fell silent. The hatches of the tank opened and the crew tumbled out, hands in air. My own men jumped out in their turn, rushing over to meet the Soviets, yelling 'Kharacho soldat! Kharacho soldat!' ('Good soldier! Good soldier!') in their elementary Russian, and embracing them. It was a hot summer day. German soldiers were soon sharing drinks, food and cigarettes with their Russian counterparts. It was a never-to-be-forgotten experience. Friendship on the battlefield, respect for an enemy regarded as an equal – in spite of everything, such feelings still existed!

LIEUTENANT COLONEL STRACHWITZ did not know the meaning of fear. In the autumn of 1942 we were holding a defensive position between the Don and the Volga, not far from Stalingrad, concealed from the Russians by a hill. We had allowed them to get within 300 metres before attacking them with the seven tanks that still remained to me. In two days our battalion destroyed more than a hundred Russian tanks. I acquitted myself creditably, but it was Strachwitz who received a decoration – the Knight's Cross with Oak Leaves. When he was posted back home, on 1 October 1942, I took over as battalion commander. This was the beginning of a painful period in the Stalingrad pocket.

On 17 November 1942, two days before the attack on Stalingrad, I was ordered to capture a small town close by, assisted by a battalion of infantry. We only had twenty tanks. The weather was frightful. I thought the plan to gain control of such an unimportant place was both dangerous and futile, and I voiced my opposition to it. As it turned out, we lost half our tanks in the operation and the infantry suffered heavy casualties, including their commander. Two days later, the Russians opened their offensive towards Stalingrad with hundreds of tanks. The moment had come for the Sixth Army to assemble its forces and break out of the pocket. But Hitler refused to hear of it and General Paulus was not prepared to initiate the procedure.

My job was to support the infantry with my last remaining tanks, five in total, out of the fifty-four per battalion at the start of hostilities. We were blinded by fog and snow, the temperature was down to below 20 degrees C. and food was running out. At the beginning of January 1943 each man was restricted to one slice of bread a day. It was inhuman to expect anybody to fight in such conditions, yet the level of morale was still astonishingly high. Up to the very end, the soldiers stuck to their blind belief in Hitler's promise to get them out of there. I knew that it was a terrible lie and that there wasn't the remotest chance of breaking through the enemy ring.

ON 20 JANUARY, my personal stroke of luck came in the form of a special mission. I received the order to report to Sixth Army headquarters to act as a courier and carry dispatches to the HQ of Field Marshal von Manstein. At that time, all those who were fit to fight had no right to leave Stalingrad. But in the final days, the high command evacuated a number of officers. I never found out to whom I owed this decision that had come like a bolt from the blue. Maybe it was General Hube, my former divisional commander, who, on leaving Stalingrad the previous day, had submitted to Field Marshal Milch a list of officers to be evacuated by air; or perhaps it was General Wenck, chief of staff of the Hollidt Army Group. At that moment, I felt very bad about leaving my men behind, and wondered how I could break the news to them. But all went smoothly and they wished me good luck, without a trace of envy. After a long wait at Gumrak airport, I clambered up with my briefcase aboard a Heinkel bomber, escorted by police who forced their way through the many sick and wounded who were trying to get on to the plane. When the aircraft eventually took off and gained height I felt I had been born again. I weighed fifty-two kilos, I was half starved, and I had neither shaved nor washed for weeks, in my filthy, torn overalls. I was returning from far, far away.

On arrival at Melipotol, on the Sea of Azov, I was taken to the headquarters of the Don Army Group to deliver my dispatch case filled with farewell letters from those trapped inside the pocket. Field Marshal von Manstein wished to speak to me.

Erich von Manstein

photograph: TopFoto

Shocked to see me in such a sorry state, his aide-de-camp, Lieutenant Stahlberg, a smartly dressed, supercilious young officer, shook hands with marked caution. He was surely wondering whether I had lice, which indeed I did. Von Manstein interrogated me for half an hour, mainly concerning the conditions which the troops in the pocket were enduring. I explained with some emotion how the majority of the soldiers of the Sixth Army still believed, with an iron will, the Führer's promise to rescue them from this hell. I mentioned the rumours that circulated and the hallucinations that haunted the overheated imaginations of the poor souls as they faced death. One man had heard the guns of the 'liberating forces', another had seen lights on the horizon or reflections in the sky. Manstein heard me out attentively but without reacting or displaying the slightest emotion.

I then reported to General Wolfram Freiherr von Richthofen, commander-in-chief of the air fleet diverted to Stalingrad, who had never even considered the possibility of organising a paratrooper drop and subsequently establishing an aerial bridgehead in such weather conditions. Richthofen lived in a personal coach on the special train that accommodated his staff. I was surprised when the carriage door was opened by an elegant young woman. This was quite extraordinary, for there were no female staff members at the front. Richthofen only granted me a few seconds, seated behind his desk in a luxurious compartment, without even inviting me to sit. 'So, you've come from Stalingrad. Thanks. I have work to do.'

I was choked with anger, exhausted and half-dead from hunger. I hoped this was the last of these formal encounters, but was informed that Field Marshal Erhard Milch also wanted to meet me. Milch had been detailed by Hitler to organise, alongside Manstein, the dropping of fresh supplies by air to the Stalingrad pocket. To my astonishment, this old Nazi proved to be far more human than all the lower-ranking officers I happened to meet throughout that day. 'My God,' he exclaimed, 'you're in a terrible state! You must get your strength back.' Milch immediately gave orders for me to have special rations. His interest in the situation at Stalingrad seemed genuine, but in the light of what I had told him, he realised that all his efforts to fly in provisions were by now too late.

AFTER STALINGRAD, it was obvious, to all those who gave it sober thought, that this was the beginning of the end. Already, back in 1941, the failure before Moscow had made me doubt victory, and I asked myself whether this war made any sense. After those long months spent on the eastern front, I became convinced – though I mentioned it to no one – that all was lost. For the regime, the war in the east was an ideological struggle against 'Judaeo-Bolshevism'. But we members of the fighting forces simply had a soldier's duty to fight against the Red Army. In 1941, Field Marshal Keitel, chief of the command of Wehrmacht, signed a judicial order exonerating German soldiers from crimes committed against the civilian population, as well as

**Hermann Göring (*left*), Wilhelm Keitel, Heinrich
Himmler and Adolf Hitler**

photograph: TopFoto

the sadly celebrated *Komissar-befehl* (commissars' memorandum), anticipating the liquidation of Soviet political commissars. On taking over command of the Eleventh Army in 1941, Field Marshal von Manstein drafted an order of the day heavily permeated with anti-Semitism.

I thank God I was never called upon to carry out these instructions. I was fortunate enough to belong to the armoured section of the Army, made up of experienced, disciplined soldiers. My unit, the 2nd Tank Regiment, had suffered few casualties in the Polish and French campaigns, preserving its peacetime character. On the eastern front, we had, as in France, strict orders to have nothing to do with the civilian population, and I was never witness to any oppressive action or massacre. We knew that the Jews had been maltreated in Germany since 1933, but we had no idea that this was in fact a programme of systematic extermination. I did not know of the existence of the *SS-Einsatzgruppen* (special detachments) who killed Jews and other categories of people behind the lines. In my battalion, several dozens of Russian prisoners worked as cooks or truck drivers. These *hiwis* (*Hilfswillige*, 'auxiliaries') were treated like the German soldiers and received the same rations.

The Army's personnel department did me no favours in sending me once more to the Russian front in the spring of 1943. In preparation for a course at the Kriegsakademie (the General Staff Academy), I was appointed to the staff of the 111th Infantry Division near Taganrog, on the Sea of Azov, in the south. This was an idyllic spot compared to the other places I had known, with a mild climate, and a landscape of apricot and peach trees surrounded by waving fields of wheat. The sturgeons of the river Mius yielded delicious caviar.

This front, initially calm, burst into action in the summer of 1943. In a massive attack, the Soviets succeeded in piercing the German lines, some 100 kilometres to the north. Russian tanks advanced and threatened our rear. The individual battalions of our division were rushed to the point of the breakthrough. Inadequately armed rearguard troops plugged the gaps. Eventually the entire division was engaged. A certain Colonel von Bülow commanded this motley collection and I was appointed his adjutant for conduct of operations. The general staff finally gave us authority to withdraw. The enemy broke through in the north and threatened our rear, along a section of river 50 kilometres away. The colonel left, ostensibly to co-ordinate the retreating units, and was never seen again.

I found myself alone in command of several thousand soldiers who lacked all fighting capacity. Once again, fortune smiled on me. A German reconnaissance aircraft flew over us repeatedly as if looking for someone. Having spotted my signals, it made a low-level run and released a canister. Inside was a sketch showing the only crossing still free whereby we could ford the river. At the last moment I managed to direct our columns in that direction and thus save the rest of our troops.

FOUR

Revenge, terror and repression

On the day of the attempt on Hitler's life, 20 July 1944, I was stationed in the operations department of Army HQ. The headquarters of the OKH was at Mauerwald, accommodated in a series of camouflaged buildings and bunkers in the middle of a forest, on the estate of Count Lehndorff-Steinort. It was one of the most beautiful landscapes of East Prussia. In the centre of the adjacent lake, the island of Uphalten was a popular destination for our rare hours of leave. When I arrived, on 1 April 1944, after my training as general staff officer at the Kriegsakademie, I came across an old friend, Colonel Johann Adolf Graf von Kielmannsegg, with whom I had fought in Poland and France in the 1st Panzer Division.

As assistant to Colonel Kielmannsegg, departmental chief of staff, I spent the whole day and part of the night in his waiting-room receiving or seeing off visitors, answering telephone calls and passing on orders. The job was hardly inspiring for a general staff officer, lacking real responsibility or opportunity for initiative, but there was a great deal happening and I gained a broad perspective of the war as it developed. One of my daily tasks was to keep the war diary, in which I had to note the events from the front and the orders and decisions of the day. I also had access to the minutes of the celebrated Führerlage, the daily meeting of the Führer's general staff, attended by the Army chief of staff, sometimes accompanied by the chief of operations.

Hitler's personal influence on military decisions was no secret to anyone. Within the department there was severe criticism of the conduct of the war, judged to be irrational and amateurish, but the Army high command was day by day losing more of its influence to the profit of the National Socialist Party. Arguments sometimes erupted, especially with Generals Schmundt, Burgdorf and Maisel, Hitler's closest liegemen in charge of Army personnel.

Events swiftly took their course – the loss of the Crimea in May, the collapse of the Central Armies, decimated by the offensive of the Red Army in June. After the evacuation of Sebastopol in early May, Hitler's fury exploded against the military leaders whom he accused of defeatism. In mid-July, the Central Group had lost twenty-eight divisions and 350,000 men, a defeat even more devastating than that at Stalingrad.

I SPENT THE whole night of 5–6 June 1944 in my office.
Around 4.30 in the morning the telephone rang. The supreme
command of the Wehrmacht (OKW), responsible for operations
on the western front, informed us that the Allied invasion had
begun. When I woke General Heusinger,* head of the operations department and my immediate superior, to tell him of the
news, this calm, controlled man replied that he had been expecting it for a long time. Greatly admired by the young officers,
Adolf Heusinger represented the very type of officer whom
Hitler mistrusted: cultured, thoughtful and intelligent, he
stemmed from the great tradition of Count Helmuth von
Moltke, chief of the general staff of the Prussian Army in the
time of Bismarck.

As we officers chatted together, the fear was that the successful landing in Normandy might turn out to be a mortal
blow, since it opened a second front on the continent, so that
the east no longer commanded priority. From now on the OKH
and OKW would each claim more material, men, weapons,
munitions and fuel. Fallen into disgrace, worn out by his incessant battles with Hitler, General Zeitzler, chief of the general
staff, was taken to hospital early in July. In utter chaos, the
Army was left without direction. Given the impasse which
reigned on every front, the military solution became even more
hypothetical. Only later did I understand how Hitler had

*General Heusinger would become the first chief-of-staff of the Bundeswehr from 1957
to 1961.

prevented the only possible alternative: the diplomatic path.

I was not a participant in the assassination attempt of 20 July 1944, nor in its preparation, but I experienced the event at very close hand. Like many of the officers, I had heard tell of the activities of General Hans Oster, head of the central bureau dealing with foreign intelligence at the Abwehr, and of the aborted 1938 plot against Hitler in which Generals Ludwig Beck, Army chief of staff, Halder, his successor, and von Witzleben, commander of the Berlin-Brandenburg region, were all involved. Nothing more, until my appointment to army headquarters where I came across the man who had facilitated my entry, some ten years earlier, into the 7th Breslau Cavalry Regiment, my cousin Wessel Freytag von Loringhoven. Aged 45, promoted colonel in 1943, he directed the section of military affairs which dealt with questions of discipline and espionage. Previously he had been responsible for one of the three divisions of the Abwehr, the intelligence service of the Wehrmacht, headed by Admiral Wilhelm Canaris. Since the late 1930s a circle had formed in the Abwehr around Colonel Oster and Hans von Dohnanyi, to explore ways of toppling the regime. The Abwehr had long been the centre of plotting against Hitler, and it had eventually come into the firing line of the SD (security service) and of the Gestapo. In April 1943, Dohnanyi and Oster had both been arrested for alleged irregular dealings in foreign currency. In February 1944, the foreign department of the Abwehr had been merged with the SS central security section, and Admiral

Canaris placed under house arrest. The noose tightened around the conspirators. Even though he never mentioned the name in front of me, I knew that my cousin was a friend of Claus von Stauffenberg, ever since they had been colleagues at the Kriegsakademie.

When we spoke for the first time, on 1 April 1944, Wessel had remarked to me that he felt he was being watched by the Gestapo. 'I shall not talk to you in an office or on the telephone, but only outdoors, well away from prying ears.' Whenever time permitted, we arranged to meet for strolls in the forest surrounding the headquarters. There it was that he mentioned to me the existence of a new plot against Hitler, without giving me any names or details, and not even admitting that he was a part of it. This news moved me greatly. At the time I was flattered to feel that this older cousin was accepting me as one of his own and I appreciated that he was sharing his secret with me. His plans fell on fertile soil. I had fought throughout the war, I had witnessed grave errors committed by our leaders, the injustice and illegality of this regime. Things couldn't go on like that and I recognised in this plot a chance to get rid of the regime.

LOOKING BACK, I found my cousin's behaviour very sensible. Unlike most of his fellow conspirators, Wessel was extremely prudent. With his experience as an intelligence officer, it was not in his nature to involve anyone without due consideration.

He had known me for a long time and he believed we shared the same ideas. He knew that if he had asked me to do anything, I would have lent him my support. In retrospect, I am certain he did not wish to compromise me, all the more since I would not have been of much use in the position that I held. Wessel did not want me to know too much. In the event of catastrophe, that would have had disastrous consequences for me. After the event, I was very grateful to him for his caution.

My cousin did not conceal from me his dissatisfaction with the manner in which the plot worked out, reproaching the conspirators for talking and writing too much. *'Weisst du Bernd, mit diesen Reichsgermanen, kann man nicht konspirieren!'* ('You know, Bernd, with these Germanic types of the Reich, you simply can't put together a plot!'), he said with that Baltic accent of his. Wessel had grown up in Russia and completed his secondary education in St Petersburg. He spoke Russian fluently, and he had a deep awareness and appreciation of that country's culture, particularly its literature and music. And from Russian history he had derived a lesson, which was foreign to the German experience, as to how to organise a plot with both skill and discretion.

ON 20 JULY 1944 I was ordered to arrange for our headquarters to be moved from Mauerwald to Zossen, south of Berlin. The Russians were getting dangerously close, about 100 kilometres from where we were located. It was a hot summer day in

East Prussia. That same evening I had to take the night train from Rastenburg to Berlin. Only some twenty kilometres separated Mauerwald from the *Wolfsschanze*, Hitler's HQ, where the explosion had occurred at around 12.45 p.m. That afternoon rumours had begun to circulate through the corridors of headquarters. Initially it was believed that the bomb had been planted by members of the OT (Todt Organisation) who worked on the construction of bunkers and air-raid shelters. In the operations department we did not know whether Hitler was dead, but we learned that our boss, General Heusinger, had been wounded and taken to the Rastenburg military hospital. On the way to the station I had asked my chauffeur to drive me there. It was a macabre scene. General Heusinger was stretched out on a bed, apparently in quite normal shape, along with five other generals who had head injuries, their faces thick with ointment for severe burns. With their white bandages and silver masks, the five high-ranking officers looked like mummies. Heusinger told me, without making any further comment, that the Führer had survived.

Next morning, on arrival in Berlin, having had difficulty in grabbing any sleep, I bought newspapers. They all mentioned Stauffenberg and reported Hitler's speech, broadcast during the night, which raged against 'a tiny clique of stupid, ambitious officers'. An announcement by Robert Ley, head of the German Workers' Front, denounced the 'blue-blooded swine'.

I was in a state of shock, deeply disturbed by Stauffenberg's

Wilhelm Burgdorf

photograph: Ullsteinbild

failed attempt. I had met him once, in 1940, after the French campaign, at the organisational department of Army headquarters. We had spoken for some twenty minutes; I don't remember what we talked about but he made a strong impression upon me. Tall and athletic, full of vitality, Claus von Stauffenberg had the bearing of a Swabian gentleman, a warm expression and a presence that I never forgot. Just like Colonel von Tresckow, another opponent of the regime, whom I had met at the start of the Russian campaign; both seemed destined for a distinguished military career.

SOON AFTER I reached Zossen, future site of the headquarters where I was to begin work, I received, around midday, a call from the OKH ordering me to return to Mauerwald by the first train. Guderian had been appointed chief of staff of the Army and I was to be his aide-de-camp. I was quite amazed and, at the same time, felt flattered. Several months after my arrival at headquarters, this post represented a fine promotion for a young major. I already knew Guderian, with whom I had fought in the French campaign and the first part of the Russian campaign. He was one of those commanders who led his troops to the scene of action in order to assess the situation for himself. He wished to have someone he knew, already familiar with headquarters routine, discreet and wholly reliable. I was pretty certain I would get on well with him.

When you took on a new assignment, the custom was for

your predecessor to introduce you and give you an idea of your new job. But on the morning of 22 July, Lieutenant Colonel Günther Smend, aide-de-camp to General Zeitzler, Guderian's predecessor, was not on hand to brief me. Nevertheless, we knew each other well. Günther had married Renate von Cossell, one of my boyhood girl-friends. We all went around in the same group and were often seen together in the late 1930s. Günther Smend was arrested on 21 July, the day after the plot.

Released several days later, he visited me in my office. It was the end of the day and Günther, worn out by the Gestapo inter-rogations, had only one wish: to rejoin his family in Westphalia. I had reserved him a seat on the night train for Berlin and accom-panied him to Rastenburg station. But things did not go as planned. On his arrival in Berlin, Gestapo men were waiting for him on the platform. Fresh accusations had been made against him, and he was rearrested and tortured. Later, I learned from Colonel von Kielmannsegg and Lieutenant Colonel von Siebert, two colleagues who had been released from the cells of Gestapo headquarters on Prinz-Albrecht-Strasse, that they wanted to find out whether his boss, General Zeitzler, knew anything about the plot. The Gestapo were particularly inter-ested in the relationship of Zeitzler and his close colleague, General Stieff. The latter had been approached by Stauffenberg on two occasions, unsuccessfully, with a view to killing Hitler, and had been arrested immediately following the events of 20 July.

Under pressure, Günther Smend had mentioned an incident to his questioners which was to prove fatal for him. On a summer evening in 1943, at the casino of general headquarters, he had been in conversation with Colonel von Kielmannsegg and Lieutenant Colonel Rathgens. The three men had reviewed the situation on the eastern front and had concluded that it was necessary to get rid of Hitler. It had been agreed that Rathgens would speak of the matter to his uncle, Field Marshal von Kluge, then commander of the Central Army Group. Kielmannsegg had saved his skin when, having second thoughts, he gave details of the conversation to his superior, Colonel Brandt, who ordered him to leave things as they stood. Because Brandt could no longer be questioned – he had been seriously injured in the explosion of 20 July and died several days later – Kielmannsegg was set free, but forbidden to take up any staff position. As for Smend and Rathgens, the simple admission of a conversation at the casino was enough to constitute high treason and condemnation to death by hanging.

On the day following the assassination attempt I thought a great deal about my cousin. Even though I did not know how deeply involved he might be in the plot, I feared he was in great danger. The arrests had just begun. As I settled down to my new job, I wondered what I could do to help him. Wessel did not know Guderian and I thought it could be useful for them to meet. On 24 July I arranged a luncheon for the three of us in Guderian's quarters. Usually very sociable, my cousin was white as a sheet and said practically nothing. Guderian was extremely friendly towards him and talked a lot, but Wessel hardly joined in the conversation. On 26 July at 7.30 a.m., I was in my office reading the letters, telegrams and notes prior to briefing Guderian, when the latter burst into the office. 'Where's your cousin?' he asked. 'I don't know, he should be in his room or his office.' 'No,' replied Guderian 'he's not there and the OKW is looking for him.' I realised at once that Wessel was going to be arrested and I volunteered to try to find him. Taking the forest path where we had previously spoken, I found him a kilometre away, lying dead, a pistol by his side and across his knees a farewell note for his wife, scribbled on a piece of paper. My cousin, one of the men on whom I had modelled my military career, had committed suicide. I scarcely had time to realise what had happened when an SS man in uniform emerged from the undergrowth, asking what I was doing there. I explained to him that the chief of staff had sent me to find my cousin; then I went back to Guderian. After listening to my report, the general fixed me with his steely blue eyes: 'Freytag, on your word of honour, did you have any knowledge of the assassination attempt?' 'No!' I replied, looking directly at him. 'It's the truth. I knew nothing of the attempt.'

After that, Guderian asked no more questions and always protected me. That was my good fortune. Had I not been his aide-de-camp, I would probably have been arrested. The simple fact of bearing the same name as one of the conspirators was sufficient to make me a suspect, all the more since we both worked at headquarters. In the days that followed, I was interrogated twice at the Wolf's Lair by SS-Obersturmbannführer Högl, head of security at the Führer's HQ in East Prussia – a terrifying person. Knowing that I enjoyed Guderian's protection, he remained courteous. I denied everything, a credible position since nobody had seen me walking with my cousin Wessel. But suspicion continued to hover over me. After the war, in 1945, a dossier in my name was actually found at the police station at Otterwisch, the place in the suburbs of Leipzig where my wife and son lived, with the following note: 'Politically untrustworthy, suspected of having participated in the plot of 20 July.' It was only much later that I discovered that my cousin had provided Stauffenberg with the detonator.

DURING THE HOURS following this dramatic episode, I wondered who would be responsible for giving a Christian burial to my cousin, who was a practising Lutheran. His wife, living in Salzburg with their four children, had immediately been arrested and taken to no. 8 Prinz-Albrecht-Strasse, the seat of the Gestapo in Berlin, where she was kept for several weeks. My cousin had said nothing to her and she had no idea that anything was afoot. Her four children, the youngest eighteen months old, had been arrested by the SS and placed under a false identity in a National Socialist children's home at Bad Sachsa, along with the children of Stauffenberg and Schwerin. Her mother could do nothing, and her brother had been arrested. I was the only one who could organise anything. With considerable difficulty I obtained the release of Wessel's body from the Gestapo. Then I needed to find a priest for the ceremony. As soon as the identity of the dead man was known, all the different religious individuals I contacted turned me down. Eventually I managed to persuade a young Protestant pastor, after long hesitation on his part. I informed a number of Wessel's friends of the time and place of the funeral – 6 August, if memory serves me – at the Protestant cemetery of Angerburg, a small town in East Prussia, near Mauerwald. All of them, under various pretexts, declined to attend, with the exception of Colonel Kleikamp, an officer of the personnel section – the only one to show any courage. The two of us, in uniform, followed the coffin, while the pastor kept on glancing left and right, fearful of being recognised. He restricted the proceedings to the bare minimum, without a word of farewell to the dead man; there was hardly the time to recite an Our Father and all was over.

During the next few days, news of the assassination attempt gradually filtered through. The entire affair appeared to have been ill-omened from the start. In his dual role of both instigator and executant, Stauffenberg could not do everything at once. In his hurry, he had not had time to prime the second bomb. His adjutant, Lieutenant Werner von Haeften, had then placed it in a rucksack. If this bomb, even without its detonator, had been carried in Stauffenberg's briefcase, the effect of the explosion would have been greater and would probably have killed Hitler. Moreover, the so-called Valkyrie operation, whereby the Reserve Army, in this case on the side of the conspirators, was to have been mobilised, was launched too late. General Erich Fellgiebel, chief of transmissions at the Führer's headquarters, had been unwilling to interfere with communications. The telephone exchange of Zossen had continued to function.

The July Plot triggered off a period of terror and persecution. Hitler's order was to track down the network to its extreme ramifications. The investigators had cause to regret that Stauffenberg and his unfortunate companions had been hastily shot on the evening of 20 July and that the leading group of conspirators, Field Marshal Erwin von Witzleben, Lieutenant Peter Graf Yorck von Wartenburg, Generals Erich Hoepner, Paul von Hase and Hellmuth Stieff, Captain Karl Friedrich Klausing, Lieutenant Colonel Robert Bernardis and Lieutenant Albrecht von Hagen had all been executed in such a hurry. With them, the principal sources that might have revealed the scope of the plot had vanished forever. Many people therefore had their lives saved by virtue of the executions or the suicide of several conspirators, such as Henning von Tresckow and my cousin Wessel Freytag von Loringhoven, who had thus cut the threads of a network that from then on would be impossible to unravel.

Claus von Stauffenberg (*top*)
Hermann Fegelein

photographs: (*top*) akg-images; Ullsteinbild

HITLER FOLLOWED THE investigation into the plot with great interest. He gave detailed instructions to Ernst Kaltenbrunner, head of the central office of Reich security. SS-Gruppenführer Heinrich Müller, head of the Gestapo, was responsible for the pursuit of every inquiry. A 'special commission of 20 July' had been set up under the authority of SS-Obersturmbannführer Georg Kiessel. Each day, at the situation meeting, Hermann Fegelein, Himmler's liaison officer, presented the commission's reports with complacent arrogance. The plot reinforced Hitler's long-standing mistrust of the general staff and the Army officers. The majority of the conspirators, in fact, belonged to this group. To my knowledge, the elder brother of Claus von Stauffenberg, Berthold, a law graduate and official at Naval Command, as well as Cäsar von Hofacker, lieutenant colonel of the Air Force Reserve and a member of the staff of General Heinrich von Stülpnagel, were the only representatives of the Navy and Air Force, where the frame of mind was very different.

I recall Hitler's reaction in August 1944 when they told him, in my presence, of the death of Field Marshal Günther von Kluge, following a heart attack. Without anyone having suggested it, Hitler concluded immediately that Kluge had taken poison, and insisted on an autopsy. Kluge had indeed swallowed a cyanide capsule on 19 August, near Metz, after being relieved of his command by Hitler who already suspected him of complicity with the conspirators and of making contact with the Allies. Actually (though this version was unknown to us), the commander-in-chief on the western front had been in touch with opponents of the regime, but refused to support them at the crucial moment. During the same period, similar rumours circulated about the dismissal of Field Marshal Erwin Rommel, likewise suspected of treason by Hitler, even though until then considered to be in the Führer's good books. That one of the bravest and most successful military commanders of the war should have distanced himself from Hitler – here was a theory that spoke volumes on the doubts assailing the high command. Convalescing after his car accident on 17 July, during an inspection of the western front, Rommel died on 14 October in circumstances that merely reinforced prevailing suspicions.*

From now on, no one could feel safe. Everyone lived in fear of being denounced. Each time the OKW arrested somebody, you never knew whether he would be seen again or whether he would be hanged. Not a day passed without the thugs of the Gestapo turning up at the OKH to arrest officers, among whom were many friends. I remained without news of them until someone heard they had been condemned to death. In case of arrest, things were predictable: execution, imprisonment or concentration camp. It was enough to recall the way in which

---

* Accused by Hitler of high treason, Rommel was given the choice of taking poison or being condemned to death by a people's court. After he had swallowed poison provided by Burgdorf and Maisel, the Führer's messengers, he was afforded the honour of a state funeral, having officially been declared dead following his accident.

the regime had treated the July Plot conspirators. In August 1944 there were radio transmissions of the first trials before the *Volksgerichtshof* (people's court), presided over by the fearsome Roland Freisler, who did everything possible to humiliate the defendants. Field Marshal Erwin von Witzleben had been deprived of his braces and belt, which forced him to hold up his trousers with one hand throughout the hearing.

The simple fact of having heard that an attempt on Hitler's life had taken place ran the attendant risk of going to the gallows. The sheer number of arrests and executions – at least those of which one was informed – clearly demonstrated the energy, the brutality and the hate with which the regime conducted its grisly work. Hitler took advantage of the occasion to impose an oath of absolute obedience on the Army. Political officials, the *Nationalsozialistische Führungsoffiziere* (NSFO), were charged with supervising the staffs.

WITHIN THE RANKS of the Army, everyone seemed to be on different wavelengths. The principal motivation of the conspirators was opposition to the irresponsibility and illegality of the regime. But many officers, especially those who served at the front, disapproved of the attempted coup. 'Prussian field marshals don't mutiny,' responded Field Marshal von Manstein famously to Rudolph-Christoph Freiherr von Gersdorff, when the latter came to sound him out during the summer of 1943. Some time before 20 July, Major Hans Albrecht von Tiesenhausen, an officer of the operations department of the OKH, had invited his twin brother Hans Dietrich von Tiesenhausen, a submarine captain, and several of his comrades, to visit him at Mauerwald. We gave them an outspoken summary of the situation on the eastern front, criticising the high command and Hitler's overall strategy. Officers of the Navy were not accustomed to hearing this kind of talk. Angered by the 'negative' outlook which evidently prevailed within our department, the submarine officers threatened to denounce us to the Gestapo for defeatism and sabotage. We had great difficulty in dissuading them.

AT HEADQUARTERS, each of us had to decide who was thinking what. You could soon distinguish the person who supported the regime from the one who was critical of it, and you adapted your behaviour accordingly, being extremely wary with the 'faithful'. As for myself, this applied above all to Hitler's immediate entourage, those whom I met at the situation conferences at the Führer's headquarters. In this environment I could speak freely only to two men, the adjutants of Field Marshal Keitel, Lieutenant Colonel Ernst John von Freyend and Major von Szymonski, with whom I had attended the Kriegsschule. With other staff officers whom I saw daily, both at Mauerwald and later at Zossen, things were different. Meeting any one of them, I knew from the start whether I could talk openly to him or whether I had to be on my guard. Even after the July incident, during the winter of 1944, comments were sometimes astonishingly open and direct. One evening, over a glass, Thilo von Werthern, a fellow officer who knew that I saw Hitler every day, asked bluntly, 'Why didn't you kill that swine?' Although not denying, in theory, that such a deed might have been possible, I explained to him that it was absolutely out of the question because I had been frisked prior to every meeting.

Nevertheless, freedom of expression was not the same after 20 July. One year earlier, in the winter of 1943, I had attended a conference at the Kriegsakademie under Lieutenant Colonel Bernhard Klamroth. This officer of the army organisational department had made remarks so critical of the high command set-up and the manner in which Hitler had treated the Army since the Blomberg affair in 1938, that I still remember it. It was dangerous for him but not one of the hundred or so officers present had exposed him. The vindictiveness of the regime, however, was unfortunately to entrap him, for Klamroth was implicated in the July Plot. Arrested on the day after the incident, in August he was condemned to death by the people's court.

The arrests took priority over the most important military matters. As the Russians drew near to general headquarters, with the eastern front 'as full of holes as an infantryman's jack-boots', to quote Guderian, the department of operations, the vital component of the general staff, found itself effectively decapitated. Colonel Heinz Brandt, joint head of the department, had died of his wounds the day after the assassination attempt. Promoted general posthumously, he was given a state burial. A funeral tribute by the chief of staff, which I had composed for him, had already been sent out to the press when the OKW suddenly cancelled everything. The Gestapo suspected Brandt of having had links with the conspiracy. General Heusinger, head of the department, who, as mentioned, had also been injured in the bomb incident, was arrested, as was Colonel von Kielmannsegg, the departmental head-of-staff. A large number of officers had similarly been put under lock and key, seriously interfering with the work of the department.

Among these was a friend, Lieutenant Colonel Bruno von Siebert, like myself originally from the Baltic region, who was responsible for relations with the Army Groups on the Russian front. Every fortnight Siebert briefed several OKH generals on the situation. A few days before 20 July, he had given them the facts. The Soviet offensive of 22 June 1944 had practically wiped out the Central Army group. Bruno von Siebert had described the situation as it was. After 20 July one of the generals who had been present denounced him for 'defeatism' and for having been involved with the plot – an accusation wholly without foundation. Von Siebert was arrested and taken to Gestapo headquarters in Berlin. Having no news of him, I plucked up the courage to go to see SS-Gruppenführer Hermann Fegelein,

Himmler's liaison officer. 'What's going on with Bruno von Siebert? He hasn't been seen since 20 July and I don't understand why he is being held so long,' I asked this unpleasant man who still retained considerable influence in Hitler's close circle. Fegelein told me he would go and see what he could do. Shortly afterwards, on his birthday, Bruno von Siebert was freed. In the autumn of 1944, at the behest of Georg Wilhelm de Hanovre – like me, a veteran of Guderian's Second Panzer Army on the eastern front – I returned to see the sinister Fegelein to ask him to intervene in favour of his brother, Prince Ernst August, arrested that August for participation in the July Plot. The prince, who had nothing to do with the conspiracy, was eventually released.

IN HIS CAPACITY of chief of staff, General Guderian received a copy of the Gestapo interrogations of arrested officers. As his aide-de-camp, I read them. I deduced that the majority of the detainees were exemplary officers, usually higher-ranking than myself. The names mentioned in their confessions, often obtained under torture, had a snowball effect and led to further arrests. It was like a storm posing a permanent threat to the entire staff – or a lead weight oppressing our individual lives.

Guderian had an ambivalent attitude towards the July Plot. Hitler had ordered him to take part in a 'court of honour', presided over by Field Marshal von Rundstedt and charged with ruling on the dismissals of Army personnel prior to their appearance before the people's court. Discharged officers accused of complicity or participation in the plot lost their military rank, could not be judged by court-martial and were hauled before the *Volksgerichtshof*. Guderian had pleaded pressure of work to be excused from taking part. He had managed to get General Kirchheim to take his place, but under pressure from Hitler was obliged to attend several sessions.

Guderian was able to save three people from death: General Heusinger, head of the operations department of the staff (HQ), General Hans Speidel, Rommel's chief of staff, and Colonel von Kielmannsegg, all arrested after 20 July. Guderian had warned Kielmannsegg that his name had come up several times in the Gestapo files, and had acted as his guarantor, but without being able to prevent his arrest. The guilt of Kielmannsegg – who had been a colleague of Stauffenberg at the Kriegsakademie and knew him well – was never proved, and he was freed before being appointed commander of an infantry regiment. Equally under suspicion, General Heusinger was a prudent man. Arrested for complicity on 22 July, no proof was discovered to support the charge. Freed by the Gestapo in October 1944, he was placed under surveillance. Guderian had recommended to the Führer that he be given command of an Army corps but Hitler remained very mistrustful and eventually made him head of the military map department. On the other hand, in spite of Guderian's efforts, General Speidel was sent to Dachau concentration camp.

General Guderian never told me exactly what he thought about the July Plot, but I sensed he felt deep pain at the ferocious measures taken against the Army. Between us, he grumbled a good deal about Hitler and the way he was running the war. In his memoirs, published after the war,* the former chief of staff declared that he had known nothing of the attempted coup. He claimed to have been opposed to the plan to assassinate the Führer, on principle, for religious reasons and because conditions held out little promise of success. Nevertheless, Guderian never explicitly professed his opposition to the attempt. His chief of staff and confidant while he was inspector general of the armoured troops, General Thomale, was none other than the brother-in-law of Graf von Schwerin von Schwanenfeld, an officer in the Abwehr, one of the most important individuals in the plot. Could this link have played a part? I don't know, but it is a possibility. The fact is that on that fateful day Guderian was on a tour of inspection and went on to his Diepenhof estate in the Warthegau, well removed from his office of inspector general of the panzer troops, in the building on the Bendlerstrasse in Berlin.

Two or three weeks after 20 July, Colonel Adrian Graf von Pückler, chief of staff of the military command of the government in Poland, wrote a letter to the Army chief of staff. In it, this old regimental comrade, just like another opponent, Rudolf-Christoph Freiherr von Gersdorf, expressed his support of the

*Heinz Guderian, *Panzer Leader*, London, 1952

authors of the plot and his indignation at the treatment meted out to them. It was a step as honourable as it was dangerous. If the letter had fallen into the hands of a Nazi, von Pückler would have been executed. When I read this letter, which placed both the writer and its recipient in peril, I advised Guderian to burn it immediately. Guderian summoned von Pückler and explained to him that the letter was 'suicidal' and that it would be better if he did not return to his post. Pückler found himself appointed head of a tank regiment on the eastern front, where unfortunately he was killed in East Prussia in the winter of 1944.

ONE PARTICULAR SCENE summed up for me the perversity of the regime in the frenzy of vengeance that followed the attempted coup. On 8 August 1944, the first of the accused had been condemned to death by the *Volksgerichtshof* and executed that same day at Plötzensee prison in Berlin. The eight victims, hung on a hook with a steel rope, suffered in agony for twenty minutes. Some days later, I was present at the daily briefing at the Wolf's Lair and was listening to Guderian reporting the situation on the eastern front when Fegelein burst into the room, brutally interrupting the proceedings, and tossed a bundle of photographs on the Führer's map table. I realised with a shock that these were pictures of the 8 August executions. Hitler put on his spectacles, eagerly grabbed up the macabre images and gazed at them for an eternity, with a look of ghoulish delight. The close-up shots of the victims' death throes were soon being passed from hand to hand. I recognised my old regimental comrade Peter Yorck von Wartenburg. His face had preserved its expression of nobility, serene and transfigured even in death. It was a terrifying moment. Guderian shrunk back and I guessed that this vile episode filled him with shame. Unable to stand the sight, I hurried from the room.

FIVE

Meetings with the Führer

THE *FÜHRERLAGE* or situation meeting eventually came
to constitute the central event in Hitler's daily life, the virtual
pivot of his military command and his everyday routine. In the
summer of 1944 this conference took place around midday, or
early afternoon. Over the months, it began later and later,
because of the communication problems that went hand in
hand with the worsening military situation. Eventually, at the
start of 1945, the meeting was held as late as 4.00 in the afternoon. Most often, it was followed by a second gathering around
midnight. These conferences sometimes went on for five or six
hours. All depended upon the Führer's whim and point of view.
When a subject gripped his attention, he would hold the floor
for hours, talking in interminable detail about the technical
features of tanks or the organisation of the front, especially
the support forces at the rear, which he aimed to maintain at
as low a level as possible. Every man capable of carrying weapons

should, in his view, be integrated into the combat troops. Hitler often criticised the gap, too wide in his opinion, between the 'supporting forces' and the 'fighting forces'.

From 23 July 1944 to 22 April 1945 the Führer's situation meetings were held at three different locations: Rastenburg, Ziegenberg and Berlin. For almost four months they took place at the Wolf's Lair near Rastenburg, in a wooden barracks similar to the one which had been destroyed in the plot of 20 July. On 20 November, when the Russians were less than 100 kilometres away, Hitler quit his headquarters in East Prussia for Berlin. The daily briefings were then held in the Führer's spacious office in the New Chancellery. This room measured 150 square metres, with ceilings nineteen metres high, the parquet floor covered with carpets. In one corner of the office, the participants gathered around an enormous marble console table used for spreading out the maps. Furniture, pictures and tapestries had been removed, sheltered from the bombing. In case of an air-raid alarm – and this happened more frequently from February 1945 – the meetings were switched to the small conference room in the bunker. At the time of the Ardennes offensive, Hitler set up his headquarters at Ziegenberg, not far from Bad Nauheim, close to the western front, where he stayed from 11 December 1944 to 15 January 1945. During this period Guderian was summoned on three occasions, on 24 December 1944, around the new year, and on 9 January 1945, the date on which I accompanied him.

Alfred Jodl (*top*) Hans Krebs

photographs: (*top*) Getty Images; akg-images

THREE GROUPS OF people attended the situation conferences: members of Hitler's entourage, representatives of the
Wehrmacht, and Party or state dignitaries. Five aides-de-camp
were included in the close circle: General Wilhelm Burgdorf,
adjutant to the Wehrmacht and head of the Army personnel
department, Major Willi Johannmeier, adjutant to the Army,
Colonel Nicolaus von Below, adjutant to the Luftwaffe, Rear
Admiral Karl-Jesko von Puttkamer, adjutant to the Navy, and
SS-Sturmbannführer Otto Günsche, aide to the Waffen-SS. The
military leaders represented the different constituents of
the Wehrmacht: Field Marshal Keitel, supreme chief of the
Wehrmacht, with his two adjutants, Lieutenant Colonel von
John and Major von Szymonski; General Alfred Jodl, chief of
the department of operations of the Wehrmacht and his two
aides, Lieutenant Colonel Brudermüller and Major Büchs;
General Winter, chief adjutant to the staff command of the
Wehrmacht; and general Heinz Guderian, chief of the Army
general staff (and later, his successor General Hans Krebs), whom
I accompanied in alternation with Captain Gerhard Boldt,
orderly officer.

The third category comprised representatives of the National
Socialist Party and the state. Since there was no foreign policy
to speak of, Ribbentrop was usually represented by his adjutant,
Ambassador Walther Hewel. When he did attend a meeting, the
Minister for Foreign Affairs remained silent. Himmler turned
up every couple of weeks, preferring to delegate his place to

SS-Gruppenführer Hermann Fegelein, his adjutant, and SS-Obergruppenführer Jüttner, his aide to the Reserve Army. The Reichsführer confined the gist of his observations to the contribution of the increasingly numerous units of the Waffen-SS.

Questions of interior security were never raised at these meetings, even when Kaltenbrunner, head of Reich security, was there. Hitler discussed such matters face to face with the individual concerned. It is hard to admit today, at a time of free speech and international communications, that for reasons relating to the nature of the regime and the operations in hand, the concentration camps and the tragic fate of the Jews were never mentioned at these meetings. Up to the end of the war, the names of the extermination camps were unknown to me. I did not have the slightest idea of the extermination process that was being conducted against the Jews.

MARTIN BORMANN, chief of Party administration, secretary and spokesman for the Führer, did not make an appearance until the second period, at the beginning of 1945, accompanied by his aide, SS-Standartenführer Wilhelm Zander. Joseph Goebbels only attended meetings during the final months, when he was enthroned as 'Reich plenipotentiary for the total war effort', and took charge of the defence of Berlin. As for Albert Speer, Minister of Armaments, he did not show up for briefings except when he wanted a private conversation with Hitler. We were also joined by Otto Dietrich, Hitler's press chief, or his deputy

Heinz Lorenz. Two stenographers of the Old Reichstag took turns at the meetings to keep minutes of the proceedings, which enabled Hitler to keep a check on every word uttered.

Other bigwigs of the regime made irregular appearances at the briefings. Hermann Göring, commander-in-chief of the Luftwaffe, only turned up once a week but was otherwise represented by General Karl Koller, chief of staff of the Luftwaffe, or by his adjutant, General Christian, husband of one of the Führer's secretaries. With Hitler's consent, the Reichsmarschall concerned himself with all manner of topics which had nothing to do with him, and held forth on them whenever his opinions contradicted those of the head of the Army. Extremely proud of his 'Hermann Göring' armoured division, he loved to follow its movements on the situation maps and to discuss its engagement with Hitler. In the autumn of 1944, when the Russians were drawing near to Rominter Heide, his hunting lodge in East Prussia, Göring boasted of his ability to defend it with his forestry rangers. Next day, it was learned that the estate had been occupied, without a shot fired, by Russian troops. Göring had not been seen at the briefings for several days. In order to avoid commenting on the repeated failures of the Luftwaffe to protect German cities against Allied bombardments, the Reichsmarschall often arranged to leave the meeting during the report on the aerial situation, leaving Major Büchs, Jodl's aide for the Luftwaffe, the thankless task of weathering the ever-continuing storm of Hitler's recriminations against the shortcomings of the air arm.

Admiral Dönitz, commander-in-chief of the Navy, was present at briefings, with his adjutant, about once a week. The rest of the time he got his liaison officer, Vice-Admiral Voss, or Captain Assmann, administrative adjutant for the Navy at the OKW, to stand in for him, making them responsible for reporting on the situation. Among other military participants, one might come across General Buhle, head of the organisational department of the OKW, and General Scherff, head of the OKW military history department. Finally, the military commanders at the front were regularly summoned to the conference for latest information or to receive instructions on the conduct of operations.

IN THE CORRIDORS of the Chancellery, while awaiting the start of the briefings, you sometimes had odd encounters. Before Christmas, for example, I was surprised to see two young women, with elegant clothes and hairdos, sauntering past. It was so unexpected that I asked my colleagues von John and von Szymonski, Keitel's adjutants, who they were. 'That's Eva Braun,' said one of them. After six months in my job I had not even heard the name mentioned. 'That's the Führer's mistress,' he added, amused at my astonishment. Among Hitler's entourage, including the officers of the Wehrmacht, it was a well-guarded secret. 'What's more,' he went on, 'her sister is married to Fegelein.' That, as it happened, I knew only too well.

'*MEINE HERREN, der Führer kommt!*' announced General Burgdorf, signalling Hitler's arrival. All of us gave the Nazi salute, Hitler shook hands with everyone present, and the meeting began. Depending on the urgency, Guderian or Jodl, reporting on the eastern and western fronts respectively, took the floor first to give the latest news from their front, referring to the large maps prepared by their staff operations departments. Colonel von Below instructed us at the last minute how we were to lay them out. Hitler did not confine himself to the standard 1:300,000 map, but often insisted on a scale of 1:100,000 or even 1:25,000 for certain sectors. During the battles of the winter of 1944–5 on the Westwall, he demanded a report based on a 1:5,000 map. All this involved a lot of extra work and blocked the high command's telephone lines, merely to obtain information of no very great interest.

With the exception of the Führer, seated in a comfortable chair in front of the map table, everyone else had to remain standing. When the briefing went on too long, the more elderly – Keitel, Guderian and Dönitz – were allowed to sit down on stools. Being in charge of the eastern front, Guderian was only concerned with a part of the daily proceedings. But on his appointment, he had received strict instructions to stay from start to finish, unlike his predecessor who had been in the habit of slipping away after giving his report and answering questions relating to his competence. Guderian complained at having to listen for hours on end to the uninteresting discussions among the representatives of the Luftwaffe and Kriegsmarine, wasting precious time that he could have spent concentrating on his own front.

MY JOB AS aide-de-camp to the Army chief of general staff was not that of a simple orderly, detailed to accompany his general, carry his documents and organise his transport. As personal assistant to the chief, I had to keep permanently in touch with the situation at the front so as to be able to react to important matters, get decisions transmitted to those in authority and immediately lay my hands on the appropriate data. In the course of the briefings, I would be told to communicate Hitler's orders by telephone. When the military situation was particularly hot, I had to seek out and transmit the latest intelligence myself.

I began my day at 7 o'clock, catching up with any news that had come in during the night. When Guderian arrived, at about 8 o'clock, I updated him with the situation at the front and handed him the reports from the different Army Groups. In order to get a first-hand impression, Guderian would from time to time receive the commanders actually stationed at the front in his office. I was also present every day at his meeting with Colonel von Bonin, head of the operations department, who came to make his report.

Before accompanying Guderian to the daily conference with Hitler, early in the afternoon, I placed the maps prepared by von Bonin in a large dispatch case which still bore the marks of the incident of 20 July. It took us less than half an hour to get from Mauerwald to the Wolf's Lair. In periods of crisis, though that was rare, we might travel by night. It was twice the distance from Zossen, south of Berlin, to the Chancellery. We had to travel through a Berlin that was half destroyed, the roads often blocked by rubble or fires. Such journeys, made twice a day, could last up to three hours. If Guderian had been attending a night briefing that ended, at the earliest, around 3.00 in the morning, he would not get back to Zossen before 5.00 a.m. To save time, Guderian often sent General Wenck, his staff adjutant, to a night meeting. This was also his way of registering his protest when Hitler launched violent accusations against his officers and the Army.

THE MAPS ILLUSTRATED to the point of absurdity the manner in which Hitler exercised his power. The Führer had abandoned the vital area of politics so as to devote himself to matters of military command. The maps reflected his obsession for detail and enabled him to get involved with the most paltry of tactical decisions, since it was he personally who issued orders for troop deployments, offensives and movements of battalions and companies. Such orders would be communicated immediately to the command posts charged with carrying them out. It was a method that aroused much discontent from top to bottom, among commanders and troops alike. On land, German soldiers paid the price with their lives.

The maps, minutely designed, with tiny flags illustrating the positions of Army corps, divisions and other formations, conveyed a pleasing illusion of the actual capacities of the German fighting forces. Looking at them, one might think that the continuous lines corresponded to divisions with fully operational troops. Those who understood the harsh realities of the front knew that these scrupulously designed maps were no more than a sham. During the last year of the war, the majority of divisions had been wiped out and were mere empty shells. Countless thousands of men were missing. Nonetheless, the same was expected of them as of divisions still capable of fighting. Data was available as to the real condition of the troops, but Hitler never took any notice. The Führer stuck obstinately to his analyses, captivated by the magic of the lines and marks on the maps.

FOLLOWING THE REPORTS of developments at the fronts, discussions between Hitler, Guderian and Jodl focused upon decisions and orders relating to the troops. It was the most delicate moment of the briefing, and the setting for the most serious controversy between Hitler and his military chiefs. The opinions and intentions of the professional soldiers were for most of the time at complete odds with those of the supreme leader. In order for him to take a personal decision, Hitler had to be informed beforehand of every offensive, retreat or withdrawal. Every proposed change had to be presented to him in minutest detail. If necessary, he would punish the alleged culprit with merciless severity and would let loose with violent diatribes against the generals, particularly those of the staff, whom he would accuse of treason and sabotage. The generals and officers present had to hear his recriminations in silence. The only ones who dared protest were Jodl and, above all, Guderian; their arguments with Hitler got more and more bitter.

Distribution of the troops was the subject that often poisoned the atmosphere in such discussions. The OKH in the east and the OKW in the west were ruthlessly competing for the assignment of the reserves in redeployment operations. On all fronts numbers had dwindled. Each command called for new troops to fill the increasing and disquieting numbers of gaps. The command structures of the OKH and the OKW tussled with each other to get more men. Hitler had to be sole judge, for example, as to whether an artillery unit or engineer battalion should be sent east or west. These Byzantine discussions, compared to others that were far more important and pertinent to the conduct of operations, culminated in endless, nerve-wracking arguments that often verged upon violence.

SIX

The Hitler I knew

When Hitler chose, he could be very agreeable. He would speak softly, in a warm, friendly tone that invariably flattered and impressed those to whom he was talking. At such times, in spite of his health problems, the Führer came across as wholly convincing, and his visitors could not help but be struck by his benevolence.

He always needed an audience to stimulate him. Approval, devotion and blind loyalty strengthened his convictions. In conversations, he deduced by instinct the attitude or potential influence of those whom he was addressing, as well as their capacity for resistance. Confronted by someone bent on contradicting him, he would immediately go on the attack, not even giving him time to finish his sentence, or cutting him short before he could say a word. The victim found himself muzzled, and Hitler saw to it that he could not open his mouth, launching into long monologues which gave full rein to his own opinions.

In military matters – an area in which he was generally considered a well-informed amateur – Hitler knew how to impose his ideas on those of highest rank. People who went to see him resolving to exercise the utmost restraint in the face of blatant errors very often came away 'converted', without having put across their point of view. On returning to their units, they soon realised that they had achieved nothing that their troops or the military situation demanded. Even those who claimed to know him best, by virtue of being with him every day at briefings, became aware that they had been manipulated. A great deal of perseverance was necessary to get him to change his mind, even partially, when things were not going his way.

Hitler would elaborate on the debate with his favourite digressions on 'miracle weapons', notably the long-range V2 rockets which he expected to be the big turning point of the war. In the field of munitions, in particular, Hitler would surprise people with his broad knowledge of detail. He enjoyed juggling with numbers, coming out with an unbelievable number of extraordinarily accurate statistics. I remember one discussion in which he mentioned the quantity of ammunition produced each month for *Feldhaubitze* (light howitzers) in 1915, 1939 and 1944. During the winter of 1944, in an animated discussion at a situation meeting he challenged an official of Speer's ministry on the very touchy matter of ammunition production for the fixed guns (*Sturmgeschütze*) installed on turretless tanks. Hitler remarked that he had defended the same point of view on a certain date in 1942 and that, at the time, facts had already proved him right. In support of what he had said, the Führer had raked up the minutes of that meeting. Everyone now present had to admit that his recollections were totally accurate.

Hitler showed astonishing creativity whenever the situation worsened. When others might have crumbled in the face of adversity, he came up with new ideas and new methods, certainly not always realistic, yet his imagination and faculties of improvisation were almost inexhaustible.

All his thoughts converged in the same direction and served only one aim: the maintenance of his power by all possible means. This was his supreme law. Anyone who dared cross his path was summarily swept aside. Despite his physical failings, Hitler applied himself personally to realising this objective with a degree of energy and relish for hard work that was quite out of the ordinary.

A shrewd autocrat, Hitler hated sharing an ounce of power and concentrated on fomenting constant divisions among his subordinates. The crumbs of authority were parsimoniously distributed so that nobody could have too much. The apparently all-powerful status of certain people proved short-lived, as Göring soon discovered. Until the start of the war the Reichsmarschall had accumulated an incredible number of functions and posts. By the end, he was merely commander-in-chief of a discredited Luftwaffe, and an instrument used by Hitler to frustrate his military opponents. Himmler's power had likewise declined during the last phase of the war after his command of the Army Group Vistula had ended in fiasco. Bormann, the 'Brown Eminence', profited from this by extending his own influence significantly, to the point of becoming the most powerful figure during the final days of the Reich.

One of Hitler's tactics was to entrust the same missions to the representatives of different organisations. Thus the *Oberpräsidenten* (super-presidents) of the provinces competed with the Gauleiters, and the Waffen-SS with the Army. Each distrusted the other and kept a sharp eye open while Hitler continued to pull the strings.

Hitler loved to send commissioners or 'Führer's delegates' to whatever place he deemed necessary. This technique permitted him to keep himself informed about the situation in any sector. Göring saw SS-Obergruppenführer Kammler, in charge of production of jet-propelled aircraft, entrusted with a mission that Hitler believed could not be performed by the Luftwaffe. It was this ambitious protégé of Himmler's who received the order to deploy the V2 rockets which were to strike at London and Antwerp. The result was unbelievable chaos. With their instinct for survival, those responsible worked against one another instead of co-operating.

Hitler concentrated extraordinary power in his hands. For him this entailed a considerable burden of work and was detrimental to the smooth functioning of the government. In a memorable lecture to the Kriegsakademie during the winter of

1943, Lieutenant Colonel Bernhard Klamroth explained to us that Hitler was monopolising no fewer than seventy-two state functions. The suppression of intermediate bodies and the refusal to delegate obliged him to take too many individual decisions, to the detriment of his function as head of state of issuing major policy directives. Given additionally the inefficiency of an overworked military high command, Hitler was simply not capable of managing both home and foreign policy. Throughout hostilities he summoned neither a council of ministers nor a war cabinet. Departments as important as finance, the economy, agriculture and labour were virtually his private domains. His 'unfortunate passion' for military affairs took precedence over other governmental duties. His cronies, who took literally his nickname of *'Gröfaz'* (*'der grösste Feldherr aller Zeiten,'* 'the greatest commander-in-chief of all time'), reinforced his self-certainty of being an infallible military genius.

NONE OF THIS prevented Hitler from treating those close to him with the utmost disdain. All the excuse he needed was a gesture or movement, without a word spoken. I can still see him before me, hunched over the map table, back arched, head sunk into shoulders, silently deliberating. This man exuded cruelty, possessing the power of life or death over every one of us.

During the last weeks of the war, the terror that emanated from him became daily more oppressive. I recollect a meeting where the question of Allied prisoners-of-war, brought back from the eastern front, was discussed in Himmler's presence. These columns of prisoners swelled the numbers of refugees, making Army movements more difficult. Hitler suddenly turned to Himmler, who was shrinking away from him, and fixed him with a menacing look. Then he made a curt reference to Allied pilots taken prisoner. All those who heard him could be in no doubt of his instructions: the prisoners were not to live. Even more agitated than usual, Himmler had turned pale, as if dogs had been let loose on him. A deathly silence followed among the company, paralysed by fear.

HITLER WAS ANYTHING but mad, in the common meaning of the term. He possessed remarkable intellectual gifts and a sharp instinct for interpersonal relations. But in many ways he was an abnormal individual, especially in his ingrained distrust of others. The Führer had no friends. Heinrich Hoffmann, his official photographer, claimed to be his crony and was treated as such. Yet this drunkard was a mere odd-job man. Hitler confided in no one and sniffed out treason and sabotage everywhere. Increasingly lonely, he lived cut off from the outside world, isolated from his people. In the first years of the war he dined, now and then, with his closed circle. By the end, his non-professional links were restricted to Eva Braun, his secretaries, his adjutants, his doctors and Martin Bormann.

THE FÜHRER WOULD accept advice from nobody, convinced he was infallible, both in political and military matters. He was an immense egoist, obsessed by the quest and then the retention of power that he had yearned for all his life. The destiny of Germany only interested him insofar as he confused it with his own. Despite all his fine words, the German people were simply a means to an end. I never heard him utter a word of compassion for the soldiers at the front, the prisoners, the wounded, the bomb victims or the refugees. Human suffering was of no consequence to him, perceived as negligible within the splendid isolation of his headquarters; and what was worse, he had no wish to see it.

One question nagged at me: why was nobody able to influence this man? Why could he not find someone to set him on the right path, to adhere to law and to honour contracts, at least to show some consideration for the sufferings of his people? The individuals whom he had most time for were the Gauleiters and Party bigwigs. They, he believed, spoke the same language and came from the same background. Towards others, Hitler harboured the most extreme prejudices. He hated people who were educated, who were steeped in true culture and tradition. The July Plot of 1944 had unleashed an inner volcanic eruption, a litany of hate-filled tirades and recriminations against the generals, the staff and the diplomats, but also against the officials and the middle classes. In the course of the final nights in the bunker, I debated this question at length with Walther

Hewel, Ribbentrop's liaison officer. 'Any understanding between him and the representatives of the elite whose job it was to influence him was impossible,' the ambassador told me, 'because he was a "petit bourgeois" (*"ein kleiner Mann"*), with all the prejudices of a "petit bourgeois".'

Hitler's physical decline had struck me when I attended a situation meeting for the first time, on 23 July 1944. This was in part the result of the treatment being given him by his doctor, Theodor Morell. Hitler had first met him in 1936 through the introduction of his photographer Heinrich Hoffmann. Dr Morell had managed to win his confidence and even, in September 1944, to secure the dismissal of two other doctors attending the Führer, Dr Karl Brandt and Dr Hans-Karl von Hasselbach. Dr Morell prescribed injections of glucose and other tonics. Before briefings or important meetings with politicians or dignitaries from abroad whom Hitler wanted to impress, Morell would personally administer such stimulants. Thus he became increasingly indispensable. In spite of the warnings of other doctors, Hitler insisted on these medicaments, which apparently had a toxic effect on his health.

Overweight and dirty, Morell was pretty repugnant to look at. Under the guise of being Hitler's personal doctor, he was essentially a war profiteer. Morell had had factories built in Germany where doubtful types of medicine were produced, such as *Russen Puder* (Russian powder), reputed to repel insects and lice. He had taken advantage of his position to impose his mediocre product on the Army, and as a result made a great deal of money. All those who, like myself, had served on the Russian front, knew that the powder was quite ineffective, with an insupportable stench for the patient.

Hitler's health problems also affected his lifestyle. Towards the end of the war, he spent practically the entire day indoors, mostly under artificial light and in the unhealthy air of the bunker, despite the ventilation installed there. He seldom emerged into the fresh air, unless to take a brief stroll, with dragging step, to play outside with his German shepherd dog.

Hitler did not get up until around midday. News from the fronts arrived during the afternoon. As soon as he rose he would begin arranging one meeting after another, receiving people from the government, the economy or the Party, who came to present reports, or perhaps studying minutes and files. During the afternoon the central event of the day was the conference on the military situation, gathering around him the high commands of the Wehrmacht and the Army. Other meetings followed in the evening. Towards midnight, a new briefing would discuss the latest intelligence from the front that had arrived in the meantime, attended by the military commanders concerned. These midnight conferences usually ended at around 3 o'clock in the morning, often later. Then came the celebrated tea hour, the only break that the Führer would agree to during his day. At this ritual gathering were his acting adjutant, one or several secretaries, a couple of his close

Theodor Morell

photograph: TopFoto

companions, such as Fegelein or Burgdorf and, occasionally, chance individuals who professed themselves his friends, like the photographer Heinrich Hoffmann and the theatre designer Benno von Arent. Conversations about art were supposed to distract him from daily affairs. Hitler then retired to his bedroom to do more work or read, before grabbing a few hours of sleep in the early hours of the morning.

THE INJURIES CAUSED by the July Plot made little impact upon his health. The heavy map table had been hurled into the air by the explosion of Stauffenberg's bomb, carried in a brief-case and placed at the leg of the table. Hitler had spun round, hit in the right arm, which by instinct he had raised in the air; but apart from his two lacerated eardrums, he had not suffered serious injuries. By 23 July he had resumed work. Yet the injured eardrums could have proved fatal. On leaving the conference room, someone had volunteered to clean out his ears with water. At the last minute he was prevented from doing so. Consulted later for treatment, Professor Carl von Ecken, a celebrated ear, nose and throat specialist at the Charity Hospital in Berlin, had explained that the introduction of dirty water into the auditory canals would certainly have led to Hitler's death. Once again, luck had been on the Führer's side.

SEVEN

Hitler versus the Army

Hitler had no other military experience apart from his time as a corporal during the First World War. He had no further familiarity with military matters until he came to power in 1933. Initially cautious, he had waited for the forced dismissal of General von Blomberg, in February 1938, to intervene personally in this field. Hitler had taken advantage of the crisis to take over the functions of the Ministry of War and to create the OKW, an armed forces supreme command, with General Keitel as chief of staff and General Jodl, at the head of the operational staff. The Führer's authority from now on extended directly to the Wehrmacht and its three branches, the Army, the Air Force (Luftwaffe) and the Navy (Kriegsmarine). The three general staffs were henceforth obedient to the orders of the head of state. Hitler had gained immediate influence over the entire Wehrmacht, yet he invariably came up against resistance within the innermost circles of the Army. Right in the middle of the war, on 19 December 1941, he had assumed supreme command of the Army, after driving Brauchitsch to resignation. This change made Hitler solely responsible for tactics as well as strategy. The different departments of the OKH (Army general staff) and the commands of the Army Groups had to defer directly to his authority. In practice, it was the chief of the general staff of the Army or of the Wehrmacht who would transmit Hitler's orders and instructions.

The complex nature of the high command structure established by Hitler resulted, as everyone realised, in the duplication of duties, and in isolation and competition between departments. The general staff of the Wehrmacht had become, at best, an advisory body, co-ordinating the three branches of the armed forces. Worse still, the OKW was in competition with the OKH. From the autumn of 1942, Hitler had given the OKW authority over the troops deployed in the Mediterranean theatre, including the Balkans, and the western front, from Bayonne to Finland, by way of Norway. Despite the appeals of the Army general staff, the OKH had found itself confined to operations on the Russian front. This duality of command was in itself quite absurd. After the Allied landing in Normandy, the 'OKW theatres of war' had assumed the same importance as the eastern front, under the responsibility of the OKH. This had led to permanent rivalry for troops, munitions and fuel, not always mitigated by the spirit of co-operation displayed by Jodl and Guderian, and their respective adjutants Winter and Wenck.

ANOTHER POLITICAL development encouraged by Hitler was the establishment of private armies, notably Himmler's Waffen-SS and Göring's land and parachute divisions. By the end of the war the numbers of these troops had greatly increased. The Waffen-SS, regarded by Hitler as more loyal than the Army, which he always mistrusted, had grown initially from four to thirty-six divisions, many of them armoured. These troops enjoyed numerous privileges and had at their disposal channels of communication with their high command. Although subject to the orders of the Army for their deployment, the Waffen-SS always did their utmost to short-circuit them. The private accusations brought by the SS against the Army commanders simply served to poison relations between the two groups and to do damage to overall cohesion.

IN ADDITION TO these continual sources of friction, resulting from Hitler's deliberate destructuring of the Wehrmacht, came the politicisation of the Army. Hitler was determined to imbue the ranks of the different services with the spirit of National Socialism; this was to be achieved through the office of Army personnel, directed by Schmundt, Burgdorf and Maisel – generals totally committed to the Nazi ideal, who had the final word on appointments. After the July Plot Guderian had been confronted by the creation of the NSFO (*Nationalsozialistiche Führungsoffiziere*), virtual political commissars charged with supervising the military on behalf of the Party. But the hostility of the majority of officers had seriously limited their influence on the activities and discipline of the troops.

The catastrophic consequences of the Wehrmacht disorganisation had helped to drive such officers into the opposition movement which had culminated in the attempted coup of 20 July. Notwithstanding the purges and transfers that had followed, a part of the Army general staff continued to question the efficacy of the high command structure and the Führer's strategic and tactical decisions. Despite the urgent need to rationalise the command, the matter was seldom raised at situation meetings. If it was, Hitler immediately curtailed the discussion. The status quo was thus maintained from December 1941 until the end of the war. This was not for want of proposals to remedy the situation. They included the re-establishment of the post of Army commander-in-chief, or at very least, the appointment of supreme chiefs for both the eastern and the western front. Field Marshal von Manstein was considered to be the most competent candidate for the former position. But Himmler's opinion of him was that he was 'a Christian and therefore unreliable', in other words unacceptable to the Nazi Party.

This disagreement concealed a deeper concern, murmured in undertones but surfacing ever more insistently: Did Hitler deserve the description of *Gröfaz*, as his critics privately nicknamed him? His experience in the trenches of the First World War had continued to weigh heavily on his military thinking.

Bernd Freytag von Loringhoven, Major (General Staff), Winter 1944–5

Photographs in this section are from the author's collection

OPPOSITE TOP Summer 1942, Ukraine; Bernd Freytag von Loringhoven, Captain, Chief 2nd Company/Panzerregiment 2

OPPOSITE BELOW Summer 1939 (before the war); (*right*) Gunther Smend, 1944 Lt. Colonel (my predecessor as aide to the Chief of General Staff of the Army). Imprisoned 21 July 1944, condemned to death; hanged 8 September 1944; (*left*) Bernd Freytag von Loringhoven

ABOVE Autumn 1941, Russia; General Guderian, Commander-in-Chief, 2nd Panzerarmee. In the back seat, Bernd Freytag von Loringhoven

OPPOSITE Autumn 1941, Russia; Generaloberst Guderian, Commander-in-Chief 2nd Panzerarmee

ABOVE Autumn 1941, Russia; Staff 2nd Panzerarmee (General Guderian) *Left to right*: Lt Colonel Bayerlein, First General Staff Officer (Ia), (later on Chief of Staff of Rommel in Africa); First Lieutenant Freytag von Loringhoven; Lt. Colonel Baron von Liebenstein, Chief of Staff; First Lieutenant Georg Wilhem, Prince of Hanover; *Foreground*: Colonel Müller, Chief Engineer

OPPOSITE Spring/summer 1943, Taganrog/Ukraine;
Bernd Freytag von Loringhoven, captain with the 111
Infantry Division (General Staff training)

ABOVE Colonel Wessel Baron Freytag von Loringhoven
1899–1944; (committed suicide 26 July 1944 after the
assassination attempt of 20 July 1944)

Bernd Freytag von Loringhoven, at home in Munich, 2005

The concept of Blitzkrieg, which he had approved at the beginning of the war, did not emanate from him but from great military strategists such as Field Marshal von Manstein. Since the initial setbacks, Hitler had resorted to his World War patterns of thinking. Faced by the staggering counter-attacks of the Red Army which had driven the German armies into retreat, he understood nothing save *'fanatischer Widerstand'* (fanatical resistance). I can still hear the way he pronounced the word *'fannatisch'*, a term he used very frequently. The repeated suggestions of the Army commanders to switch to a technique of mobile defence, and to give up pieces of territory, were systematically ignored, in keeping with the same maxim of linear defence. Arguments that underlined unsustainable losses and overstretched resources made not the slightest impact upon him. Bloody battles of encirclement had destroyed the flower of our men and shattered the morale of our troops. By the end of the war, the eastern front, particularly the northern sector, consisted merely of a series of islands surrounded by the enemy. By order of the Führer, some of the best divisions had been stationed in Courland (southern Latvia), in East Prussia and West Prussia, while the Volkssturm (people's militia) and Hitler Youth defended the capital of the Reich.

FOR THEIR PART, the soldiers directly concerned had learned to leave aside all sentiment in order to reach an objective judgement. Only the *'Beurteilung der Lage'* (situation evaluation), based upon minute examination of data concerning each of the protagonists, could enable the military to take a logical decision to carry through an operation with all the means at their disposal. This method was quite alien to Hitler's thinking. He and his generals simply did not speak the same language. Hitler relied on intuition and his personal feelings, such as prestige, hate and revenge.

Hitler always tended to underestimate the enemy and overestimate his own troops. He concocted his own subjective vision of reality and stuck to it, come hell or high water. Facts were discarded as 'defeatist' when they demonstrated too clearly the strength of the enemy. Hitler would reiterate at situation meetings that Russia had run out of steam and that her Army had long since collapsed. When anyone dared point out that one Russian division comprised 10,000 men, he replied curtly that its numbers did not amount to more than 2,000 men. At the same time, Hitler acted as if the German divisions were still full of fight, ignoring the fact that they were severely weakened, often reduced to a few hundred men.

THE RUNNING BATTLE between Hitler and his generals, and his deep distrust of the Army, led inevitably to an atmosphere of conflict. Hitler had created chaos in the high command so as to reduce the power of the Army, only too aware of the danger that it posed for him. When there was still time, in 1938, the Army had hesitated to act. The military leaders had been much criticised for failing to think in political terms but, under the Weimar Republic, the Reichswehr had been schooled precisely along those lines. Its head, General von Seeckt, had strictly forbidden his officers to get mixed up in politics. What had perhaps been a good recipe for the Weimar Republic, with its continuous political quarrels, had proved to be a fatal practice under the Nazi regime.

Confronted by politicians who were expert manipulators, the non-political senior officers of the Reichswehr had been only too easily manoeuvred. When Hitler had decided, in agreement with the Army, to eliminate Ernst Röhm and to reduce the influence of the SA on 30 June 1934, he had also taken the opportunity to get rid of General Kurt von Schleicher, former Reich Chancellor, and General von Bredow, in the course of the 'night of the long knives'. This double political assassination had caught the Army leaders completely unawares, leaving them incapable of reacting.

The same scenario was repeated at the beginning of 1938 with the Blomberg-Fritsch affair. General Werner von Blomberg had been forced to quit his post as Minister of War by reason of his marriage to a woman of dubious reputation. General von Fritsch, commander-in-chief of the Army, had been placed on reserve after defamatory accusations of homosexuality. Hitler had stepped in to take over personally the direction of the Wehrmacht, without appointing a successor to the Ministry of War. To cover up the scandal, the Führer had embarked upon a complete overhaul of his armies. The generals, without turning a hair, had accepted the humiliation brought down on their commander-in-chief and the grave infringement of their rights. Once again Hitler had found the means to consolidate his domination of the Army. He realised that he could do what he wanted with the generals who were not of any consequence in his political planning. Most of those whom I knew were brave men and worthy leaders of troops, concerned with the safety of their soldiers. But they complied with Hitler's orders and were numbed by his rhetoric. Not until the collapse of the eastern front were they to recognise how they had been hoaxed.

The soldier's duty of unconditional obedience had its roots in the traditional relationship of the king and his officers. But the respect for one's superior, to whom complete responsibility had to be entrusted, now had a disastrous effect. Reservatio mentalis (closing one's mind) made obedience easier. By virtue of this tradition, the present-day military leaders deferred to the head of state, who thus discharged them of their responsibility to history.

EIGHT

Servants and schemers

Hitler's entourage afforded him the audience he required. These were people who, whether by conviction or opportunism, found him agreeable and created around him the environment that he needed in order to assert himself. Hitler detested face-to-face encounters and it was almost impossible to obtain one. He feared making a concession that he would subsequently regret. He wanted his actions and decisions known to all in his inner circle. Martin Bormann, head of the Party Chancellery and secretary to the Führer, controlled all access and was employed to prohibit direct contact. Stocky, with a bull's neck, and sparse, wiry black hair, Bormann had the odd habit of shrugging his shoulders and gazing at you with shifty eyes. Apart from the final months, he was rarely seen in Hitler's headquarters. Yet nothing escaped the Brown Eminence, always skulking in the shadows, close to Hitler, like a spider in its web. A tireless worker, Bormann heard and watched over everything happening around him. The absolute confidence that Hitler accorded him gave him unrestricted access and the opportunity of speaking alone with the Führer. The way in which he spent his time, modelled on that of Hitler, allowed him to go about incognito late at night, when there was less activity in the Chancellery bunkers. Bormann was a declared enemy of the Army, which he regarded as an obstacle to the supreme power of the Party. According to National Socialist propaganda, the iron will of the Party, under the leadership of the Führer, not the Army, would bring final victory to the German people.

Goebbels, whom I saw only during the final days, was entirely different. Unlike Bormann, *petit bourgeois* and uneducated, with all the complexes and hunger for power common to this class, the Minister of Propaganda had intelligence and a certain presence. He was one of the very few not to crack under the enormous psychological pressure of the last days in the bunker, as was not the case with Bormann. Goebbels remained loyal to Hitler to the very end.

IN MIDSUMMER 1944 Himmler was probably the most powerful person after Hitler. One of the major beneficiaries of the failed assassination attempt of 20 July, the Reichsführer-SS had secured access to the military sphere by becoming commander of the Reserve Army, a function that he added to those of chief of police and Minister of the Interior. In December 1944 Hitler had appointed him commander-in-chief of the Upper

Martin Bormann

photograph © Corbis

Heinrich Himmler

photograph © Corbis

Rhine Army Groups, apparently encouraged by Bormann, who wanted to get him away from Berlin. Himmler suffered from the complexes of one who had never exercised true military command, in contrast to several of his aides, festooned with decorations. Too young to serve in the First World War, he had joined a military unit in 1918, but had never been sent into combat. Now responsible for the front between the Palatinate and Switzerland, Himmler had reinforced his weakened and demoralised soldiers with reserve troops of the SS, who had managed for several weeks to hold a bridgehead near Colmar, on the left bank of the Rhine, something that pleased Hitler greatly.

When the eastern front, along the entire length of the Vistula, collapsed in January, Hitler decided to appoint Himmler, against the wishes of Guderian, as commander-in-chief of a new group of Vistula armies. The Führer considered Himmler the only man capable of mobilising the reserve troops still available in the Reich. Himmler had in fact managed swiftly to collect together a strange medley of police, parachutists, Waffen-SS and *Volkssturm*. This improvised organisation, however, faced the Russian onslaught with an assortment of troops that lacked cohesion and had minimum fighting capability. Guderian was outraged to see such an important post entrusted to someone who was totally inexperienced. To make things worse, Himmler had chosen SS-Brigadeführer Lammerding as his chief of staff, a respected soldier but without any staff experience. His adjutant, Colonel Hans Georg Eismann, from the general staff, had, in fact, deputised for him in this capacity.

The weight of responsibility quickly proved much too heavy for Himmler, who was a complete failure in his role as commander of the Army Group. In mid-February, after an unforgettable argument with Guderian, Hitler eventually agreed to give General Walther Wenck – and not Himmler – direction of the counter-offensive on the Oder, but the loss of Pomerania, and thus the link with East Prussia, could not be avoided. One month later, the Reichsführer-SS was relieved of his command. His prestige suffered greatly from this episode and his position alongside Hitler went into free fall, so much so that he made fewer and fewer appearances at the Führer's headquarters. The last time I saw him, he seemed to me paler, more distracted and agitated than usual. At the time, I was wholly unaware of the full scope of the atrocities committed under his orders, but I believed already that the shadows of the innumerable dead whom he had on his conscience must be pursuing him and depriving him of rest.

ONE OF THE MOST sinister figures around Hitler was SS-Gruppenführer Hermann Fegelein, Himmler's liaison officer. The multiple functions of the Reichsführer enabled this arrogant, corrupt dandy to interfere in everything, from interior policy to police matters and military affairs. During situation briefings he would interrupt people, including Hitler himself, in a manner verging on insolence.

The son of a Bavarian cavalry sergeant from the First World War, Fegelein had built his career thanks to his talents as a horseman. The Waffen-SS had bought him horses of quality with which he had won a number of competitions for the SS. During the war he had been made commander of an SS cavalry brigade and sent, in the winter of 1941, to the region north-east of Smolensk. There Fegelein had been decorated with the Knight's Cross. Later, his brigade was transformed into a division and he had been awarded the Knight's Cross with Oak-Leaves. Assigned in due course to the Führer's headquarters, this incorrigible egoist found the means to get his Oak-Leaves with Swords, a decoration obtained thanks to his close friend General Schörner, the prototype of a Nazi general. Almost at the same time, Hitler awarded him the Silver Bar, an extremely rare decoration, given in recognition of having participated in a large number of closely related actions.

Fegelein talked the jargon, the slang of a porter in a Munich brewery. His unbridled ambition drove him to exploit, with all the cunning of a cheeky peasant, every means to his advantage. His cleverest stroke had been his marriage, celebrated at enormous expense in the spring of 1944, to Gretel Braun, sister of Eva Braun, the Führer's mistress. This alliance had made him one of the most powerful individuals in Hitler's intimate circle. A sworn enemy of the Wehrmacht and its 'reactionary' spirit,

Hermann Göring

photograph: Getty Images

he never ceased to express his offensive opinions of the Army and its corps of officers. Once, in a conversation with Jodl, after a conference which had gone on until dawn, Fegelein had described the officers of the general staff as 'traitors'. Jodl had coolly snubbed him.

HERMANN GÖRING, dwindling, dying star of the regime, had the appearance of a clown, dressed like a general in operetta, with a white uniform in midwinter and jackboots of violet leather fitting over his knees. The eccentricity of the commander-in-chief of the Luftwaffe, rouged and perfumed, fingers covered with rings, made us giggle. His pompous life style and the debacle of the German Air Force had utterly discredited him. At the situation meetings Hitler criticised him harshly for the poor performances of the Luftwaffe, but he never dared replace him.

Army chief of staff and highest-ranking officer in the military hierarchy, Field Marshal Wilhelm Keitel allowed himself to be totally dominated by Hitler. Deep down, he was undoubtedly an honest, pleasant man; but his intellectual gifts were at best limited and the burden of responsibility entailed by his position was too much for him. I always had the feeling that Hitler put him into a blue funk and that he was forever trying, like an apprentice, to placate his dreaded employer. His submissive behaviour was almost shameful. It was shocking for a young officer like myself to see Keitel, a field marshal more than sixty years old, turn up at the double whenever Hitler summoned him.

At briefings, where he should have been the principal adviser, he lent a ready ear to everything Hitler said. I never heard him express the slightest personal opinion. He was, however, an extremely conscientious administrator, who worked every day until late at night. Methodical and meticulous, he had a boundless admiration for Hitler, clearly stupefied at his master's agility of mind and imagination. His nickname of *Lakeitel* (the lackey) unfortunately suited him only too well. Guderian scorned the servility of the OKW chief of staff. On the only occasion that I had visited Guderian at his estate of Deipenhof in the Warthegau, he showed me his flock of sheep, of which he was very proud. 'Don't you think that he looks like Keitel?' he remarked ironically, pointing his finger at one of two rams which, in all honesty, did bear some resemblance to that most loyal of all Hitler's military servants.

MUCH LATER, in captivity, General Kurt Zeitzler, Guderian's predecessor, told me how he had tried, in late November 1942, to obtain the go-ahead from Hitler to attempt a breakout by the Sixth Army from the Stalingrad pocket. At a meeting of a select few, including Keitel and Jodl, Zeitzler had pleaded eloquently for such an operation. Visibly impressed by his presentation, Hitler hesitated and asked Jodl and Keitel for their advice. In contrast to Jodl, who gave a vague response, Keitel argued unequivocally against a breakout from Stalingrad by the Sixth Army. The city was a symbol and had to be held. The Volga, Russia's main economic artery, must remain blocked. Keitel was merely repeating the arguments that had already been voiced by Hitler himself. Given this endorsement of his own views, Hitler had refused to sanction Zeitzler's proposals. The Sixth Army had remained in Stalingrad until it was annihilated by the Red Army.

GENERAL ALFRED JODL was a completely different type, always calm and considered. The words he uttered were deliberate and carefully chosen. The head of the Operations Office of the OKW was far too intelligent to fall under Hitler's spell. In the last years of the war his viewpoint on military operations seldom coincided with those of the Führer, whom he never feared to contradict. That would put Hitler in a very bad mood and he would not shake hands for several days. But neither of the two wanted to put an end to their relationship. During the final months, Jodl expressed himself freely in front of Hitler, as few others would have dared to do. The closer the end approached, the greater became my respect for him. I believed him to be, like Keitel, wholly dedicated to Hitler, by virtue of his long service with the OKW. Actually, Jodl harboured a greater measure of intellectual independence than I ever imagined.

GENERAL WILHELM BURGDORF, Hitler's principal adjutant, played a highly pernicious role on the Führer's staff. He had succeeded General Schmundt, who had died of his wounds from the July Plot, having previously been his adjutant. Since the departure of Brauchitsch in December 1941, this post had been fused with that of head of the Army personnel department. Schmundt had been enjoined to lend a National Socialist proclivity to the officer corps. Burgdorf was expected to continue this task, all the more strongly after the July Plot. More brutal than Schmundt, Burgdorf subscribed body and soul to Hitler and the Party. Uncultivated, coarse and vulgar, he embodied perfectly the Nazi clique. His setback at headquarters and his mediocre career with the armed forces had nurtured his resentment against the generals and members of the staff.

Burgdorf battled energetically against tradition and elitism, seeking at any price to impose the Nazi ideal of *Volksofficier* (people's officer) within the officer corps, and was nicknamed *Vomag, Volksoffizier mit Arbeitergesicht,* (people's officer with the head of a labourer). Apart from any consideration of competence, the *Volksoffizier* was expected to be politically reliable and to stick to the Party line. The recruitment process of the *Nationalsozialistische Führungsoffiziere* (NSFO) – virtually political commissars charged with watching over the National Socialist attitudes of colleagues – had been planned but never materialised, simply because not enough fanatics could be assembled. In future, the regime sought a solution through a radical change within the corps of officers. For this task Burgdorf found the most eager support from Himmler, Fegelein and Bormann. The Army was now in the most absurd of situations, in which there was no discussion about important changes in command positions between the head of the personnel department and the generals, but only with these three individuals, serving the troops with a *fait accompli* by order of the Führer.

ONE NOTABLE EXCEPTION to this chapter of failures was Burgdorf's close relationship with General Ferdinand Schörner. During the period of the Reichswehr, under the Weimar Republic, this self-styled practising Catholic had taken the opportunity to advertise his membership of the church to advance his career in Bavaria. After Hitler's seizure of power, Schörner had thrown his faith overboard, together with all other kinds of useless baggage, in order to become an enthusiastic Nazi. Hated by the troops, the general had the reputation of being a bloodthirsty monster, known for his brutality and draconian forms of punishment, even for minor infringements of military regulations. During the winter of 1942–3, Schörner commanded an Army corps in Finland. In the freezing night air, he hunted down his own soldiers, guilty of wasting fuel by driving about in a vehicle without authorisation. In the course of one of these nocturnal patrols on the icy roads, he had observed in front of him a black car, and had overtaken it to force it to stop. 'You're looking mightily surprised, you stupid old country cop,' came the cry, in Bavarian dialect, from the passenger in the car, General Eduard Dietl, his superior in rank, commander-in-chief of the Finnish-German Army. Having become persona grata with Hitler, Schörner appeared frequently at his side, unlike the other senior military leaders. As a consequence of his visits to the Führer's HQ, he struck up a firm friendship with Burgdorf, Bormann and Fegelein.

Burgdorf's activities had earned him the fully merited name of *Totengräber des deutschen Offizierkorps* (gravedigger of the German officer corps). Burgdorf and his adjutant, General Ernst Maisel, an odd-job man who put on grand airs, played a major role in the bloody repression that followed upon the events of 20 July. Eyewitnesses told me about the sessions of the court of honour set up by Hitler to rule on the dismissal of officers suspected of having been involved in the plot, prior to their judgement by the Volksgerichtshof. Burgdorf and Maisel had proved to be even more fanatical and merciless than Kaltenbrunner and his Gestapo assistants. Even those who had been released by the Gestapo, particularly staff officers, were pursued by the hatred of Burgdorf and banished from their former posts.

NINE

The rush to the abyss

Appointed chief of the Army general staff on 21 July 1944. Guderian was not the Führer's first choice. Hitler thought of giving the post to General Buhle, replacing General Zeitzler, but this officer, a dedicated Nazi though without battle experience, had been injured in the July Plot. At this time, the situation at the front was critical. The Central Army Groups had been defeated. Russian troops were nearing the eastern border of Prussia approximately 90 kilometres from the Wolf's Lair headquarters. So Hitler turned to Guderian because of his experience of the Russian front and his reputation as a tank specialist.

By the late 1930s Guderian was numbered among Hitler's disciples. In his view, the Führer had the vision to have recognised the importance of tanks in modern warfare, contrary to the generals of the older generation. Guderian complained a lot about General Beck, who was still fixated on the static strategy of the First World War. But Guderian's relationship with Hitler deteriorated rapidly following the start of the offensive against the Soviet Union, so much so that the champion of armoured warfare was abruptly relieved of his command of the Second Panzer Army on 26 December 1941. Guderian had to wait until February 1943 to gain another appointment, when Hitler made him Inspector General of Panzers. With an anxious eye to the future, the Führer offered him, as a sign of gratitude, the estate of Diepenhof, in the Warthegau, a region of Poland annexed by the Reich.

The unexpected appointment of Guderian occurred in difficult circumstances. His predecessors, Halder and Zeitzler, had resigned after lengthy disagreements with Hitler about the conduct of operations. Despite such unpromising auspices, the partnership between Hitler and Guderian began well. Hitler showed a measure of deference towards Guderian, who suffered from heart problems. He even invited him to sit down during situation briefings and suggested he consult his personal physician, Dr Morell, which Guderian declined. For his part, Guderian made sure to keep his ears open. Within weeks, under the pressure of accumulating events, this surface civility disappeared, due to the ever more frequent disagreements between the two men.

THE RED ARMY offensives made a direct impact upon the fragile network of the Reich's alliances. At the beginning of August 1944, Turkey announced the breaking-off of relations with Germany. Finland, which had fought for so long against the Soviets, sent out signs of wavering after the resignation of President Risto Ryti, on 1 August of the same year, to be replaced by Field Marshal Gustaf von Mannerheim. Visits by Schörner and Keitel failed to prevent the new Finnish head of state signing an armistice with the USSR on 19 September.

On 5 August, Marshal Antonescu was received by Hitler at the Wolf's Lair in the hope of strengthening links with Romania. Guderian took part in the discussions, with Keitel and Ribbentrop. To my great surprise, I heard him deliver a report of the military situation, in excellent French, to the Romanian dictator. Antonescu had appeared to us to be quite au fait with the information from the front, but he was deluding himself in his evaluation of the situation inside Romania when he assured us of the unconditional loyalty of his people, and of his own army to the German Reich. On 20 August, when the Soviets launched their attack against the Southern Ukraine Army Groups, the Romanian troops deserted en masse and turned on their former allies. Three days later, Antonescu was overthrown in a *coup d'état*, before being condemned to death by a people's court and executed shortly afterwards. Meanwhile, King Michael of Romania hastened to declare war on Germany.

Early in September it was the turn of Bulgaria to change sides. The moment Soviet troops crossed the frontier, Bulgaria, too, deserted the camp. A communist putsch toppled the monarchy and Sofia was occupied by the Red Army. After this new reverse,

German domination of the entire Balkans region was directly under threat. German troops were forced to abandon Greece, Albania and southern Yugoslavia. Guderian had not succeeded in getting what he wanted, namely the transfer to the eastern front of the eighteen divisions which continued their hopeless battle against Tito's partisans.

The consecutive defections of Romania and Bulgaria to some extent weakened the alliance with Hungary. At the end of August 1944, Guderian was sent to Budapest, bearing a letter from Hitler to Admiral Horthy, the head of state. I travelled with him aboard a Focke-Wulfe Condor – a speedy plane for its time – escorted during the journey by four fighters. Guderian emerged deeply doubtful after his head-to-head conversation with the Hungarian regent. The admiral had received him courteously but had given him the impression of being on the verge of terminating his alliance with Germany. Our real host in Budapest was General Vörös, chief of the Hungarian general staff, who proved particularly friendly. Several weeks later, in October, Vörös paid us a courteous visit to our headquarters at Mauerwald, in East Prussia. The general assured us of his loyalty and Guderian rewarded him with the gift of a Mercedes. A few days after that, on 15 October, Vörös used his new limousine to surrender himself to the Soviets, who already occupied a large part of his country. Next day, by order of Hitler, Horthy was overthrown and replaced by a government led by the Hungarian fascist Ferenc Szálasi. The German occupation was to last until the fall of Budapest in February 1945, but the Reich had by now lost its Hungarian ally.

FROM THE ECONOMIC viewpoint, the situation was hardly brighter. In a note addressed to Hitler at the beginning of September 1944, Albert Speer sounded the alarm. There were shortages of raw materials and the low level of fuel stocks was keeping aircraft grounded and restricting troop movements. Eventually, armaments production would dry up. Speer's conclusion was unambiguous: at this rate, the war would be lost within months. Far from prostrating Hitler, this news strengthened his resolve to take the initiative. Since he had nothing to lose, the Ardennes offensive would be his final bluff. He needed to gain time. A surprise victory over the Allies would allow him to negotiate a separate peace with them. The employment of new weapons, an increased number of aircraft and the fragmentation of the coalition opposing Germany would put him in a strong position to confront the Russian offensive expected in January.

Stemming from this same alarmist prediction, General Guderian drew diametrically opposite conclusions. The chief of the Army general staff favoured doing everything possible to check the Soviet offensive and avoid the loss of the historic provinces of the Reich and of Silesia, the last major industrial zone located beyond the range of Allied air forces. Guderian believed that this rescue process was possible on condition that

Courland (in south-western Latvia), Norway, northern Italy and the Balkans were evacuated in order to reinforce the eastern front with the considerable number of mobile forces thus freed for action. Guderian wanted, above all, to rescue the German troops encircled by the Russians in Courland.

Allergic to any idea of withdrawal, Hitler reckoned, in contrast to Guderian, that an evacuation of Italy would simply speed up the rate of Allied air bombardments of Germany. The loss of Balkan mineral resources and Hungarian oil would be disastrous for the economy of the Reich. The continuation of the German presence in Norway and Courland was essential for the resumption of submarine warfare envisaged by Dönitz. The grand admiral had always adhered unflinchingly to the Nazi ideal and had the ear of Hitler. Dönitz claimed that he needed the Baltic Sea as a 'field of manoeuvre' for the training of new submariners. The German presence in Courland also served to tie down the enemy in the Baltic. Actually, the importance of the Kriegsmarine had dwindled considerably after the destruction of most of its battleships, such as the *Bismarck* and the *Tirpitz*. Since the breaking of its secret code transmissions by the British, the U-boat fleet had suffered heavy losses. Submarines could be likened more and more to suicide commandos, which did not deter Dönitz from entrusting their crews with new missions, many never to return.

In addition to simple divergences of opinion as to which strategy to pursue, very different philosophies separated the two men. Hitler refused utterly any thought of surrender. It was necessary to fight to the finish, even if it entailed the destruction of the German people and their leader. For Guderian, on the contrary, the duty of every German patriot was to prevent the country's destruction, even at the price of capitulating to the Allies. Even though hope was slender, everything had to be attempted to bring about an end to the war. An agreement with the Allies would perhaps prevent eastern Germany falling into the hands of the Russians.

ON ALL FRONTS, from north to south, from east to west, Germany was experiencing setbacks, yet in late summer of 1944 something of a lull occurred. The highly energetic but unprepossessing Field Marshal Walter Model had gradually managed to plug the enormous breach that had opened since the collapse of the Central Army Groups. The Soviet forces had nevertheless continued their advance. The Northern Army Group had been forced to withdraw from Estonia and the northern part of Latvia where the ports of Libau and Windau, two vital points of access to the sea, were situated. The German Army in East Prussia had tried to protect a land route to the troops stationed in the Courland peninsula. In September 1944 my former battalion commander, Colonel Hyazinth Graf von Strachwitz, had won distinction by re-establishing a corridor between Courland and East Prussia, as leader of a small panzer division. But this brave action merely had a short-term effect. A new Soviet thrust had subsequently isolated the German troops completely. From east to west, the enemy was getting dangerously close to the frontiers of the Reich, although their offensives were losing intensity. The German Army succeeded in containing its adversaries, forcing them into lengthy and costly battle. The moment had arrived for Hitler to play his trump card.

THE OBJECTIVE OF Operation *Herbstnebel* (autumn fog) was to cross the Eifel massif and the Ardennes, then advance through Belgium to reach the Channel and take Antwerp. To win his bet, Hitler relied upon the Sixth SS Panzer Army, led by SS-Oberstgruppenführer Sepp Dietrich, and the Fifth Panzer Army of General Hasso von Manteuffel. The high command managed to keep it absolutely secret. All communications were forbidden. Among those involved, only a few officers knew of the plan and the enemy did not expect an operation of such scope.

The Ardennes offensive presented Guderian with a *fait accompli*, at the very time he wanted to reinforce the eastern front to block the progress of the Red Army. Since he was responsible for operations in the east, Guderian found himself in a weak position vis-à-vis Jodl, head of the operations bureau of the OKW, when it came to obtaining troop reinforcements and logistics. Guderian had no faith in this offensive. The Army chief of staff considered it far too ambitious, taking account of the forces available, doomed to failure by the crushing aerial superiority of the foe, and not even guaranteed an adequate supply of fuel. The operation resembled an act of despair when it would surely have been more worthwhile to shore up the eastern front in expectation of imminent Soviet attacks. Never had a major German offensive been so ill prepared.

Guderian's fears proved justified after the deceptive speed of the first few days of the German advance. The difficult terrain, bad weather, shortage of fuel and loose command of the Waffen-SS divisions had got the better of the operation. The Allies, however, recovered swiftly from their surprise. As soon as conditions permitted, they stepped up their aerial attacks on the German forces. On 26 December, after the withdrawal from Bastogne by the Americans, it was clear that the action begun on 16 December had ground to a halt. The diversionary offensive launched on 1 January in northern Alsace merely augmented the futile losses. On 8 January Hitler ordered the panzers to retreat.

Nicknamed *Brausewetter* ('roaring storm') by his subordinates, a warm-hearted and cultured man, Guderian was one of those rare generals who evidently had no qualms about standing up to the Führer. During the Ardennes offensive, Guderian made three visits to the *Adlerhorst* ('Eagle's Nest'), near Ziegenberg, Hitler's chosen headquarters from mid-December. Each time he pleaded in vain for the reinforcement of the eastern front. On the first occasion, on Christmas Eve, Guderian again requested the transfer to the east of the divisions stationed in the Courland peninsula in Latvia or, at least, the units withdrawn from Norway. Hitler rejected the proposal, based on the estimations of the strength of the Red Army by General Reinhard Gehlen, head of the *Fremde Heere Ost* (eastern military intelligence) of the OKH. He judged it to be simply a bluff, 'the greatest piece of trickery since Genghis Khan'. Jodl realised that the offensive had failed to produce the hoped-for results but insisted on the need to 'retain the new-found initiative in the west'.

Without forewarning Guderian, the Führer had personally ordered the transfer to Hungary – the other current bee in his bonnet – of the Fourth SS Panzer Division, then stationed north of Warsaw, to relieve Budapest, where the German troops were under siege. Returning to Ziegenberg on 1 January 1945 to plead his case once again, Guderian ended up obtaining the reinforcement of four divisions taken from the western front and Italy.

HITLER HAD YET another obsession. In Hungary, Budapest was about to be lost and the Russians were advancing towards the Plattensee. Hitler wanted to lift the threat to the oil supplies located to the west of Hungary, near Zistersdorf in Austria, by regaining the regions between Drau and the Plattensee as far as the Danube. The Führer proposed to cross the Danube and break through the Russian lines south of the Carpathians. When I heard him developing this crazy idea at a situation meeting, the thought crossed my mind: did this man wish to destroy the German people? Carrying out such a plan would entail a number of practical difficulties. The only existing railway leading to Hungary was vulnerable to Allied air attacks. The transfer of five divisions of the Sixth SS Panzer Army would take five or six weeks, much longer than a transport to the east where several railway lines were available.

AT THE BEGINNING of January 1945 I had accompanied Guderian on a tour of inspection of the eastern fronts in Hungary and Poland. We had met General Wöhler, commander of Army Group South, at his headquarters in the castle of Ester-haza, on the border between Hungary and Austria. At Cracow, General Harpe, commander-in-chief of Army Group A, deployed between the Carpathians and Warsaw, had pointed to the rein-forcement of Soviet forces at the Vistula bridgeheads, between Baranov and Pulaky. All indications were that the offensive was imminent. The general proposed evacuating sections of front so as to pull back twenty or so kilometres, out of range of the Soviet artillery, forming a shorter and more easily defen-sible line. Intelligence from General Gehlen noted that a large concentration of tanks signalled the preparation of a major offensive.

When he returned, on 9 January, Guderian went to see Hitler once more at Ziegenberg to beg yet again for reinforcements. At the same time, he conveyed to him the evaluations of Gehlen and Seidemann. Maps and graphics illustrated the highly unfavourable balance of strengths in the Vistula region. Guderian pointed to the aerial reconnaissance photographs of General Seidemann, commander of the Luftwaffe, showing that approximately 8,000 Soviet aircraft were assembled at airfields close to the Vistula and East Prussian fronts.

Göring then interrupted Guderian, banging his fist on the map: 'Don't believe him, *mein Führer*, the Soviets no longer have so many planes. They're simply decoys!' Uninformed of the situation but, as ever, anxious to please Hitler, Keitel rapped his fist at the same point on the map, saying: 'The Reichsmarschall is right!' Beside himself with rage, Hitler described the estimations of the military intelligence services as 'completely idiotic'. Whoever thought them up deserved to be confined in a madhouse. Guderian replied that the person in question was General Gehlen, one of the finest of staff officers, and that if Hitler proposed locking him up, he, Guderian, should join him. Once again, Hitler turned down all suggestions of withdrawal and troop transfers.

Three days later, 12 January, the Russian offensive was launched. A torrent of armed strength surged westward over the immense space lying between the Carpathians and the Baltic Sea. The remaining German Army corps and, indeed, entire armies, vanished completely, swallowed up without having made any contact with one another. Our only intelligence came from the Soviet radio, which broadcast the names of prisoners and German generals who had fallen on the battlefield. The Soviet military leaders had learned a great deal. They had copied our method of concentrating troops in the centre, followed by a swift forward thrust, without bothering about the flanks. Moreover, the Soviet forces were swiftly and boldly exploiting their success. Warsaw and Cracow soon fell into their hands. As Guderian feared, the Russians occupied Silesia. The enemy advanced as far as Posen and Danzig, before pausing briefly on the Oder. This catastrophe led to many thousands of German victims, military and civilian. In the snow and cold, a vast displacement of population ensued. Long columns of refugees fled along the roads, by horse, by car, on bicycles or on foot; and all the time death and disease hovered over them.

RELATIONS BETWEEN HITLER and Guderian grew daily more venomous. On 15 January, before quitting his western headquarters at Ziegenberg, Hitler gave the order to transfer the Grossdeutschland Panzer Corps from East Prussia to the neighbourhood of Kielce, in Poland, where the Red Army was threatening to break through. Guderian refused to comply. Not only would it be impossible to execute such a manoeuvre in time to check the Soviet troops, but it would at the same time weaken the defence of East Prussia, at the very moment when it was in imminent danger of Soviet attack. Hitler was not prepared to cancel the order; the troops had been waiting several days in the railway sidings. After the return of the Führer to

Berlin, on 16 January, the situation meetings were characterised almost daily by angry confrontations. Guderian was furious to learn from Jodl that the Sixth Panzer Army of Sepp Dietrich, having withdrawn from the Ardennes, would be sent to Hungary. It was during that period that Hitler entrusted Himmler – against Guderian's advice – with the command of the new Army Group Vistula, formed in haste to halt the Soviet advance.

At the beginning of February, Hitler and Guderian discussed the need for an operation in Pomerania. To retain a corridor between East Prussia and Pomerania, Guderian favoured a thrust east of the Oder in a southerly direction. In his opinion such an action would make it possible to protect Berlin and gain time. After a lunch, where the drink flowed freely, with the Japanese ambassador, General Oshima, a staunch friend of Germany, at his residence in Tiergarten, we had returned to the Chancellery to attend the meeting. That morning, in the car, between Zossen and Berlin, Guderian had confided in me his intention of once again raising the question of retreat from Courland. 'This time,' he had burst out excitedly, 'I'm really going to tell him!' Guderian wanted permission to move the twenty-two divisions stationed in Courland. The general went straight to the point, arguing his case passionately, and the discussion soon turned sour. The two men confronted each other, with Guderian holding his own against the Führer. Nobody else dared interrupt. Swayed by the reluctance of Dönitz to support the evacuation, Hitler refused to concede anything. Two hundred thousand men therefore remained immobilised until the surrender in May 1945.

Guderian then returned to the fray, toning down his plan by proposing a single attack southward from the Baltic in order to consolidate the defence of Pomerania and avoid the isolation of the Second Army. Time was of the essence, since Russian reinforcements were pouring in daily on the Oder front. Guderian urged rapid action and proposed entrusting direction of the offensive to his adjutant, General Wenck, in preference to Himmler, who provided growing proof of his incompetence with every day that passed. The Reichsführer SS was only too aware that his military reputation, already much compromised, would be ruined by another fiasco, and did everything in his power to delay the inevitable. At the briefing of 13 February, Guderian made it clear that he wanted the operation to commence within two days. Supported by Hitler, Himmler immediately raised objections, claiming that the transport of fuel and munitions was far from complete. The debate then shifted to the question of command of the counter-offensive, and once more erupted into reciprocal fury. Pale as death, Hitler paced up and down the room, coming to an abrupt halt to hurl accusations at Guderian. Himmler could easily have had him arrested. Then, against all expectation, Hitler informed Himmler, quite out of the blue, that General Wenck would come that very evening to his headquarters to take over direction of the offensive. Unfortunately, Wenck was seriously wounded in a car accident on 17 February, returning to his own head-quarters following a night-time meeting with the Führer. The operation, which had begun quite promisingly, now ended in failure.

In Guderian's judgement, the collapse of the Ardennes counter-attack, the success of the great Soviet offensive in mid-January and the loss of Upper Silesia signified that the end of the war was near. The defeat of Germany was comprehensive. The only hope of avoiding total destruction of the country and its seizure by the Soviet Union would be a 'political solution'. Guderian had no illusions. The chief of staff, ever a realist, knew that since the Casablanca conference in January 1943 the Allies had been demanding of Germany no less than unconditional surrender. But perhaps the western powers could be persuaded that it was in their interest to prevent the Russians dominating Germany in the post-war period by accepting the surrender of the western regions of the Reich so as to enable her to defend her eastern frontiers. Given the desperate military situation, Guderian was keen to encourage the top individuals in the regime to convince Hitler of the need to negotiate an armistice on the western front.

BACK IN JANUARY, the arrival of Dr Paul Barandon, the new liaison officer between the Ministry of Foreign Affairs and the Army, had already given Guderian the opportunity to request an audience with Ribbentrop. On 25 January 1945, Guderian met the minister to propose a joint representation to Hitler. The military situation was dire, the Russians could, in his view, be at the gates of Berlin within a few weeks. Ribbentrop appeared taken aback by this prediction but nevertheless reaffirmed his loyalty to the Führer and, aware of the latter's hostility to negotiations, refused to support Guderian. Although he assured him that he would remain silent about their conversation, Ribbentrop lost no time in telling Hitler of it. That same evening, at the situation meeting, Hitler lectured Guderian: 'When the chief of the general staff goes to see the Minister of Foreign Affairs and informs him of the situation in the east with a view to obtaining an armistice with the West, he is nothing more nor less than guilty of treason!' But he took no action against him.

GUDERIAN THEN ATTEMPTED, in late winter, to mobilise Albert Speer. He had come to know the Minister of Armaments in his capacity of Inspector General of Panzers and they had worked together on tank production. The two men liked each other. Guderian was impressed by the efficiency with which Speer continued to handle production by the armaments industry in spite of Allied bombings. Speer had a fairly realistic idea of the situation and had not concealed from Hitler his opinion that the war was lost. When, on 19 March 1945, Hitler signed a decree on 'measures of destruction in the territory of the Reich', Guderian and Speer joined forces to prevent its application. Speer shared Guderian's viewpoint but their conversations reached no concrete conclusion.

At the end of March Guderian made a third approach, this time to Himmler. He knew that his close collaborator, SS-Brigadeführer Walter Schellenberg, head of foreign intelligence at the central office of Reich security, had made contact with the West through the intermediary of Sweden. On 21 March, during a walk in the Chancellery gardens, Guderian asked Himmler if he would agree to go with him to the Führer in order to propose opening negotiations. 'My dear general,' replied Himmler curtly, 'it's still too soon for that.' Like the other props of the regime, the Reichsführer feared losing the favour of his chief and intended to play a lone hand.

INCAPABLE OF ADMITTING to the slightest fault, Hitler sought scapegoats for every setback. For each reverse on land, experienced officers lost their command, accused of incompetence or treachery. At Army headquarters, Guderian, his adjutant General Wenck and Colonel Bogislaw von Bonin, head of the operations department, worked in exemplary harmony. During the Gestapo inquiries which followed the incident of 20 July, Bonin's name had allegedly been linked to Colonel Schultze Büttger, arrested and then executed for complicity in the plot. There had been no follow-up; Bonin had not been concerned and had kept his post. Hitler, who read avidly the most

Albert Speer and Adolf Hitler

photograph: Getty Images

important Gestapo reports about the conspiracy, had memorised all the names mentioned in the proceedings. On 16 January, in late afternoon, at the height of the Soviet offensive, Colonel von Bonin went to find Guderian in his apartment to inform him of the latest developments at the front. The chief of staff was getting ready to leave for the situation meeting in Berlin, together with General Wenck. The fall of Warsaw seemed imminent, if not accomplished. Army Group A had lost contact with the four battalions charged with defending 'Fortress Warsaw' and Soviet soldiers had already been sighted west of the city. The news seemed so credible that Guderian and Wenck had not even bothered to verify it. Bonin suggested a withdrawal of the Army Group to a new line of defence, a measure promptly approved by Guderian.

On his arrival at the Chancellery, Guderian explained the situation, and was immediately interrupted by Hitler who demanded where this information had originated. 'From the Army Group,' replied Guderian. 'Who actually told you?' insisted Hitler, becoming more and more furious. 'Bonin,' said Guderian. Hitler was already crying treason when a telegram arrived from the OKH. The commander of the 'fortress' was still in the city but the situation was untenable. He and his troops were preparing to leave. 'Arrest them all!' yelled Hitler. 'Fortress Warsaw has to be held at any cost!' The Führer's order, immediately communicated by radio, could not prevent the German withdrawal. The situation was obvious to everyone except Hitler. If the command had followed his instructions, the German troops, vastly inferior in numbers and under-equipped, would have had no choice but to surrender.

Beside himself with rage, Hitler would not let the matter drop. For several days he would return to the subject of Warsaw in all its ramifications. Next day, the retreat from Warsaw occupied the entire briefing, overshadowing all other developments, unquestionably more important, on the various fronts. Who said what? Who was to blame? At the operations department of headquarters, Lieutenant Colonel von Christen, chief of the Army Groups section, had been the first to hear of the news before transmitting it to Lieutenant Colonel von dem Knesebeck, who had himself informed Colonel von Bonin. On discovery of this chain of command, Hitler gave the order to arrest the three officers. As soon as the name of Bonin had been mentioned, Hitler had made the link with 20 July and smelled out 'conspiracy'.

I had remained at OKH headquarters at Zossen, waiting by the telephone. I feared the matter must have repercussions. Around midnight Guderian rang, sounding very tired, to tell me he had tried everything but that Hitler was not budging on the arrest order. Soon afterwards, General Ernst Maisel, deputy chief of the Army personnel department, burst into my office accompanied by two lieutenants armed with automatic pistols. He was a small, fat, unpleasant man. 'Where are these three officers?' he barked, showing me the arrest warrant. I volunteered to go to look for them, and after some hesitation he agreed, on my word of honour to bring them back. It was about 2.00 in the morning. I went to knock on the door of Bonin's room; he was lying stretched out on his bed in uniform. 'I was expecting you,' he said calmly when I explained the reason for my visit. Given no choice, we felt quite powerless, yet bound in unison. Before going back to Maisel, I took time to drink a glass of Sekt with von Bonin, von dem Knesebeck, von Christen and all the officers of the operations department.

AT THIS CRITICAL MOMENT of the war, Guderian was himself subjected to interrogations by Ernst Kaltenbrunner, head of the security service of the Reich (RSHA) and Heinrich Müller, head of the Gestapo. A key department of headquarters had been deprived of three experienced officers. Brought to the Prinz-Albrecht-Strasse for questioning by the Gestapo, von dem Knesebeck and von Christen were released after two weeks, but without recovering their posts at headquarters. Both were sent to lead a regiment at the front and the former was killed in Hungary, a few days after taking up his command. Von Bonin was sent to the Dachau concentration camp where he met individuals such as Léon Blum, General Speidel, General Halder, General von Falkenhausen and Pastor Martin Niemöller.

AFTER THE MID-JANUARY rout, the Führer dismissed, one after another, three generals. Held responsible for the collapse on the Vistula, General Joseph Harpe was replaced at the head of Army Group A by Ferdinand Schörner. It was then the turn of General Hans Reinhardt, commander of the Centre Army Group, who had made the mistake of evacuating the coastal positions after the Soviet breakthrough of 26 January, and of General Friedrich Hossbach, commander of the Fourth Army, who had retreated from his position when threatened with encirclement.

Even the SS were not immune to the Führer's vindictive nature. In March, when the divisions of Sepp Dietrich's Sixth Panzer Army were making a fighting retreat on the Danube, Hitler instructed the elite Leibstandarte Adolf-Hitler division to remove its 'Adolf Hitler' insignia, but this humiliating order was never applied. After the failure of the counter-offensive in Pomerania, Himmler was himself, on 20 March, relieved of his duties as commander-in-chief of the Vistula Army Group. Some days previously, I had accompanied Guderian when he met Himmler to try to persuade him to give up his command. At the moment when Russian tanks were breaking through in Pomerania, the Reichsführer SS had taken sick leave at the SS hospital of Hohenlychen, twenty kilometres north of Berlin, cared for by his personal doctor, SS Professor Karl Gebhardt, *

* Karl Gebhardt, co-ordinator of experiments on human beings in the concentration camps, was condemned to death in August 1947 by the Nuremberg tribunal.

for what appeared to be nothing more than a heavy cold. During a two-hour private meeting, Guderian explained to him diplomatically that he was, according to all evidence, burdened by too many responsibilities and that he could not, at the same time, assume command of such an important Army Group. He suggested giving it up. Himmler wished for nothing better but hesitated to speak about it personally to Hitler. So Guderian grasped the opportunity and volunteered to do so on Himmler's behalf. That same evening, Hitler accepted Guderian's proposal to appoint General Heinrici in place of the Reichsführer SS.

Another officer to be targeted by Hitler was General Reinhard Gehlen, head of the *Fremde Heere Ost*, in spite of the fact that he was doing meticulous work, with excellent results. His predictions as to the intentions of the enemy had often proved to be very accurate. Initially wary, Guderian came to appreciate the precision and reliability of the work carried out by Gehlen's service, and frequently depended upon on its findings, particularly during the winter of 1944, prior to the huge Russian offensive of mid-January. At his request, General Gehlen was present several times at the situation conferences. Hitler, however, did not trust the staff intelligence work, which he regularly labelled 'defeatist', and lay in wait for an appropriate occasion to sack Gehlen. At the beginning of March, Gehlen announced that a Russian offensive across the Oder against Berlin was imminent. Actually, the Russians only attacked two weeks later, in Pomerania. Gehlen was immediately dismissed, the Fremde Herre Ost denounced as incompetent and its numbers significantly reduced.

The noose tightened around Berlin. On 15 March, our Zossen headquarters was heavily bombarded. One bomb hit the concrete building that housed the operations department; General Krebs, Guderian's deputy, was wounded, as were several staff officers. I was having lunch with my aide-de-camp, Captain Gerhard Boldt, when we heard the air-raid alarm on the radio. We ran full tilt towards the bunker. The ground shuddered from the shell-bursts as we slammed the iron door behind us at the last minute.

Guderian's position was becoming more and more precarious. His wrangles with Hitler culminated brutally on 28 March in his dismissal. On 21 March, after the daily briefing, Hitler took Guderian aside to enquire after his health. 'I have been told your heart problems have returned. You need to rest for a few weeks.' It was said in such a friendly tone that Guderian had suspected no duplicitous intention. He had replied that it was difficult for him to leave, since his two deputies were unavailable, General Wenck not yet recovered from the injuries from his car accident, and General Krebs wounded six days earlier during the bombardment.

The matter was merely postponed. Hitler found the opportunity the day after the failure of the counter-attack on Küstrin. On 27 March, the Ninth Army had attempted unsuccessfully to extricate the troops encircled there. At the afternoon meeting

Hitler hurled unjustified charges at General Theodor Busse, commander of the Ninth Army. These criticisms were greatly resented by Guderian, who had leapt to the defence of the accused officer. Summoned the following day together with Busse, Guderian expected a stormy session. Once again he defended Busse who had used up every available shell. Then he brought up Hitler's refusal to authorise the retreat of the Courland divisions for the defence of Berlin. Hitler literally jumped up, pale as death, and began to pace up and down the large office of the New Chancellery where the meeting was being held. He heaped reproaches on Guderian for the failure of the Pomeranian offensive, the defeatist attitude of the staff and the continuous sabotaging of his plans. Guderian replied by pointing to the Führer's own responsibility for the short-comings of the command. The storm that had been gathering for so long now erupted like a hurricane. 'Don't get yourself so excited, *mein Führer!*' begged Burgdorf in a trembling voice, trying to get him to sit down.

I was afraid Guderian would get himself arrested. The Bonin affair was still uppermost in my mind. I just had to find a way to ease the tension. It occurred to me to slip away to telephone General Krebs at Zossen, explain the situation to him and ask him to furnish me with an excuse to interrupt the conference, which he immediately understood. I returned to the meeting room to tell Guderian that Krebs wanted to speak to him urgently. Krebs kept Guderian on the phone for ten minutes.

When the chief of staff came back into the room, the pressure had eased a bit. Jodl was outlining the situation on the western front. General Winter, Jodl's adjutant, led Guderian aside into a corner of the room so that the lion-taming could continue. Finally, Hitler ordered everyone to leave, apart from Keitel and Guderian, who informed me of Hitler's proposal a few minutes later: 'General, for the sake of your health you must take six weeks of convalescence immediately. By then the situation will be absolutely critical and my need for you will be urgent.'

OFFICIALLY GIVEN LEAVE for health reasons, Guderian was duly replaced by General Hans Krebs. Aged 46, and thus ten years younger than Guderian, Krebs was an intelligent, resourceful man with a quick mind and a capacity for hard work. He had risen rapidly through the ranks as a staff officer but had never commanded troops. As chief of staff to Field Marshal Model, his visits to Hitler's headquarters had enabled him to cement relationships within the Führer's entourage. Krebs was not a Nazi, but he was an opportunist and had the advantage of being a friend of General Burgdorf, a former classmate at the Kriegsakademie, who was a dedicated National Socialist and very close to Hitler. Before reaching the top post, Krebs had replaced General Wenck, Guderian's deputy, after his car accident in mid-February. From then on, he had alternated with Guderian at the situation meetings. Krebs had soon won Hitler's goodwill, his dry humour being appreciated by the Führer. Very flexible and adaptable, Krebs took care not to make his opinions known and never confronted Hitler. Whether it was in his nature to make light of things or whether he had no illusions about his chances of influencing Hitler, I do not know. Krebs frequently remarked to me that the war had long since been lost. He was too intelligent not to see where this was all leading us. When I asked him if I could return to join the panzer troops, Guderian's successor replied: 'Freytag, I'm requesting you to stay with me. I am not going to look for anyone else, seeing that the war will be over in four weeks.'

EVENTS GATHERED PACE. In the west, the Allies broke through and headed for central Germany. The Model Army Group was encircled and destroyed in the Ruhr basin. At the beginning of April we expected the Soviet offensive at any moment. Together with Krebs I continued to make the daily journey from Zossen to Berlin for the briefings, which were now held in the bunker. Because of the bombardments we had to divert from many streets closed to traffic.

On 13 April 1945, when the death of Roosevelt was announced, Goebbels' euphoria contaminated Hitler. For several days, the Ministry of Propaganda embarked on a repetition of the 'miracle of the House of Brandenburg', whereby the death of the Tsarina Elisabeth had saved Frederick II from disaster in the Seven Years War. But, as usual, reality dissipated all illusions. The much-feared Russian offensive got under way on

16 April. During the first few hours, the Russian advance was modest but, as soon as they had sufficiently broadened their bridgeheads on the Oder, the front collapsed and the Army Groups of Marshal Koniev drew near to southern Berlin. Russian and American troops linked up on the Elbe. The division of Germany into two parts appeared imminent. The discussions of the regime's hierarchy now focused on the question of evacuating Berlin. In view of the coming assault on the capital, the 'national redoubt' of the Bavarian Alps certainly offered the best possibility of continued defence. Those closest to Hitler urged him to leave for Berchtesgaden, but he remained hesitant. In the event of the Reich being cut in half, two headquarters had been established as a precaution: one for the northern zone was to be headed by Grand Admiral Dönitz. The other, for the southern zone, would come under the orders of Field Marshal Kesselring.

AT HEADQUARTERS we never had any idea where we would be sent next. On the morning of 21 April, the Russians captured Baruth, south of Berlin. Some forty T-34 Soviet tanks were heading towards Zossen. Summoned to the rescue, the handful of tanks from the Tank School at Wünsdorf could do little more than slow up their progress. For lack of fuel, the Soviet tanks came to a halt a dozen or so kilometres from the headquarters. The following day, around midday, Burgdorf telephoned the Chancellery for authorisation to transfer the OKH to Eiche and the OKW to Krampnitz, two barracks complexes near Potsdam. The OKH hurriedly abandoned their concrete quarters and underground tunnels which represented the hub of the German war machine. Some hours later, Russian soldiers penetrated the largest and best protected telephone centre in the world, buried forty metres below ground. No one was prepared, or had the time, to blow up the installations. As luck would have it, in the course of one of their final sorties, German aircraft had mistakenly targeted an OKH convoy and there had been casualties. This headlong stampede by generals and colonels took on the guise of a desperate flight rather than an orderly, disciplined evacuation.

TEN

High fever in the bunker

It was 22 April 1945, around 8.00 in the evening, following the situation meeting which had gone on for the whole afternoon in the *Führerbunker*. The stunned participants now climbed up the stairs to the *Vorbunker*,* where the adjutants awaited the end of the conference. In a voice full of resignation, General Krebs told me the news: he had received the order to remain in the bunker, as the Führer's personal adviser. The news petrified me. I had no choice. As his aide-de-camp, I was condemned to stay by his side. For anyone who understood the military situation, Hitler's decision was my death warrant. For some time I had seen this conclusion drawing nearer. It had not escaped me that, after his entry into Hitler's close circle, Krebs had gradually won his regard and trust. Several days earlier, as we drove around in the car, I had warned him not to play out the last act in company with Hitler.

* Ante-bunker or upper level of the bunker.

Now it was too late, and I could do nothing to change things.

For Krebs, as for myself, the order came as a complete shock. That same morning we had hurriedly moved our headquarters from Zossen to Eiche, a former school for officers near Potsdam, while the OKW travelled to Krampnitz. Krebs had expected to remain with the combined general staff, the result of the expected fusion of the OKW and the OKH. The only solution appeared to be to evacuate Hitler by plane southward to Berchtesgaden, from where he could preside over the final act of the tragedy. But the Führer had decided to stay in Berlin. Why on earth should Hitler choose Krebs, the army chief of staff, to accompany him into the bunker, in preference to his old cronies Keitel and Jodl, who had been at his beck and call since the start of the war? That remained a mystery. Hitler had only known Krebs for a couple of months. But the atmosphere in and around the Chancellery had become so irrational that this relative newcomer might perhaps provide Hitler with the vague hope of a miraculous solution.

Krebs now described the dramatic meeting. The leading personalities of the Reich, except for Göring and Himmler, were crowded into the tiny space of the bunker conference room to hear Jodl and Krebs attempting to explain the truly catastrophic state of affairs. The Russians and Americans would shortly complete their link-up on the Elbe, the provisional demarcation line anticipated under the Yalta agreements. In the south, the Americans were continuing their rapid advance as the writing on the wall took on an ever clearer aspect in Italy. In the north, the Americans and the British had taken up positions on the Elbe. To the east, the Oder front had collapsed. Right through the meeting the bad news kept coming in. Soviet troops had succeeded in breaking through into the northern suburbs, and Krebs had been forced to admit that the long-awaited attack of the SS corps led by SS-Obergruppenführer Felix Steiner had not taken place. The encirclement and fall of the capital of the Reich were inescapable. Having kept quiet for some time, eyes fixed on the map table, the Führer broke the silence to order everyone to leave the room apart from Keitel, Jodl, Krebs, Burgdorf and Bormann.

He then lashed out violently at the entire world, all those in whom he had placed his trust and who had betrayed him, principally the officers of the high command. The war was lost, he tearfully confessed for the first time, but he would stay in Berlin to direct the defence of the city and end his life rather than fall into enemy hands. Hitler had at last recognised the full extent of the catastrophe, but was never to admit his own responsibility.

In front of the silent generals, something totally strange and unexpected now occurred. Bormann, head of the Party Chancellery, spoke up in defence of the Wehrmacht and the military, calling all those there to witness. The Führer's secretary affirmed that the generals present and the great majority of officers and soldiers had done their duty to the end, in conformity with their oath and in a praiseworthy manner. It would be unjust, therefore, to accuse them of treason and saddle them with responsibility for the defeat. This intervention caused astonishment, coming as it did from a schemer who had long nursed his secret hatred for the Wehrmacht. Imminent disaster had suddenly dragged the truth from the lips of an inveterate liar! Bormann went on in a more normal tone, insisting that all hope was not yet lost. There still remained Wenck's Twelfth Army, Busse's Ninth Army and, above all, Schörner's Army Groups. His remarks helped to relax the atmosphere. Each man made his little speech to persuade Hitler that it was not yet the end of the world.

It was enough to allow him to recover his spirits and to start building new castles in the air. Schörner would attack the flank of the Russians advancing from the south on Berlin. Wenck was to reassemble his forces and march on the capital. The Luftwaffe would throw all its aircraft into the fray. Keitel and Jodl had full powers to co-ordinate all the forces available outside the capital. The staffs of the OKW and the OKH were finally fused. Once more, Hitler's power of suggestion produced its effect. Far from deserting Hitler at the moment he was cracking up, his faithful few did all they could to help him escape from a hopeless situation.

IT WAS THE BUNKER or Bavaria. While I was settling in with Krebs at the New Chancellery, others were packing their bags for Berchtesgaden. On the night of 22–23 April, my first in the bunker, I observed the amusing sight of rats leaving the sinking ship. Any excuse would do to slip away. I can still see tubby Dr Morell, slumped like a sack of potatoes in the Führer's waiting room, there to beg permission to leave the bunker. SS-Obergruppenführer Schaub, aide-de-camp and former chauffeur to Hitler, likewise appeared to have nothing more urgent on his hands than to run away. That the stenographers and secretaries should be evacuated by air from the Chancellery seemed only right. But that 'trusties' such as Morell and Schaub, who had spent their time proclaiming their loyalty to the Führer, should now want to distance themselves from him, seemed to me to be downright indecent. Hitler, who had decided to stay put, exhibited, as it happened, astonishing generosity. All those who asked to leave were allowed to go.

THAT NIGHT, I was standing by chance at the foot of the bunker staircase when I saw Magda Goebbels arrive. She was a beautiful woman, very elegant, and was followed down the stairs, in single file, by her six children. I felt deep foreboding at the sight of their frail figures, sombre clothes and pale, anxious faces. What an idea to bring these innocent creatures into such a dreadful place! Nothing would happen to them were they to be sent to Bavaria. Like the others, these children risked never coming out from here alive.

Even the *Führer Nachrichten Abteilung*, (communication battalion), had found a pretext for leaving their post. On the morning of the 23 April, when I tried to get in touch with the OKW, it was obvious they had all vanished into thin air. There was no longer a single Army radio set in the bunker. We had to make do with one of the Party transmitters, which did not work too well, and with codes completely different to those of the Army. We had to call upon military command in Berlin to establish a radio-telephone link with the OKW. Communication proved possible thanks to two transmitters fixed to a radio tower at Berlin-Halensee and to a captive balloon, positioned over Rheinsberg. This system did not allow us to communicate directly with the Wehrmacht commands. Any rare intelligence that we received came from the OKW, with whom links were very poor and intermittent. Talking on this short-wave connection required considerable physical effort. You had to concentrate very hard to make out the words. Moreover, communication was often interrupted in the middle of a sentence.

I SHARED THE work with Gerhard Boldt, my orderly officer, who had joined me in the bunker. Boldt was in charge of Berlin and its surroundings, calling up the sector commanders or their staffs. If that proved impossible or inadequate, he

Paul Joseph and Magda Goebbels

photograph © Corbis

made use of a directory to ring at random private numbers. If anyone answered, Boldt would ask them what was going on around them. If it was a Russian voice, it was easy to draw the conclusion.

For my part, I gathered information relating to the other theatres of operation. We didn't know much about what was happening in southern Germany, Bohemia or Italy. The OKW, which had moved from Krampnitz to Rheinsberg on 24 April, knew even less. To obtain intelligence and transmit orders, I had the idea of intercepting radio messages from Reuters in London, which were systematically heard and re-transcribed by Heinz Lorenz, the acting press officer – one of those rare individuals, apart from Boldt and myself, who did any actual work in the bunker. We found ourselves in a grotesque position whereby any situation report given to Hitler was based largely on information derived from an enemy radio. Far from adhering strictly to Chancellery protocol, daily business seesawed in an atmosphere of chaotic improvisation, with much more linited, informal meetings.

Day after day we marked up the maps for Krebs and Hitler. When important news came in, I went at once by way of the *Kannenberggang** to the Führer's bunker and showed it to Krebs and Hitler. The latter listened for most of the time without saying anything. What interested him, above all, were the

---

* The underground passage between the two bunkers, named after Arthur Kannenberg, Hitler's *Hausintendant* or majordomo.

movements of the troops in charge of the defence of Berlin. Hunched over the map table, the Führer would lose himself in conjectures, moving armies and divisions which no longer existed, and issuing inapplicable orders that we were increasingly powerless to transmit. All units stationed between the Elbe and the Oder were to march on Berlin. Steiner was to regroup in the region of Oranienburg and Lichtenwalde in preparation for a counter-attack. Busse would hold his positions on the Oder. The Twelfth Army, in position on the Elbe, opposite the Americans, was to make an immediate about-turn to attack the flanks of Koniev's formations in the neighbourhood of Potsdam and break through in our direction. This did not include the troops under the command of the general of Army Corps Holste, due to attack Berlin from the west. The truth was that not only were the units concerned incapable of carrying out the orders streaming from the bunker, but also that their commanders ignored them.

On the morning of 23 April, Krebs made a final visit to check on the orders that he had transmitted personally to Wenck during the night. Wenck's Army could rely on young soldiers, operational and motivated, thanks to their membership of the Hitler Youth, but their numbers were down to three divisions. The rest comprised a hotchpotch of miscellaneous troops without any cohesion, randomly assembled from new recruits picked up in the streets. If General Wenck were to advance on Berlin, it would not be to rescue Hitler but to open a corridor between the capital and the Elbe, enabling General Busse's Ninth Army, together with civilians, to escape the Red Army.

THAT SAME DAY, the Russians broke through towards Dallgow-Döberitz, virtually cutting off the gateway to the west. Their advance extended north-west of Berlin. Throughout the day of 24 April, Hitler continued to place his hope in the offensive by Steiner, who had received the order to attack the Army Groups of Marshal Zhukov. Personally involved in the preparations, he kept himself continuously informed of the state of play. SS-Gruppenführer Fegelein had been dispatched the previous evening to Himmler to get reassurance that the SS were sending Steiner all possible reinforcements. Several times, in my presence, Himmler's liaison man had offered to take personal command of the offensive. Fegelein manifestly was seeking a way to quit the bunker of death to save his skin. To achieve this, he had no qualms about casting doubt upon Steiner's military qualities, while boosting his own. But Hitler, who still had his wits about him, had turned down the offer, making sure to summon him as soon as he returned from his mission. Obviously he had more confidence in Steiner than in his future brother-in-law, who was more often than not under the influence of alcohol.

With his three divisions almost out of steam, Steiner's group eventually launched their attack, but given the Russian superiority, it came to nothing. Increasingly edgy, Hitler plied

Krebs incessantly with questions to which we had absolutely no answers. That evening, when it was clear that the attack had failed, the Führer heaped reproaches on Steiner and the high command, accusing them of disloyalty and incompetence. Steiner was dismissed and replaced by General Holste, but made a pact with the latter to retain his command.

Everything was becoming more and more surreal, detached from reality, here in this underground world that never saw the light of day. I was living in the midst of a crowd of strangers, inextricably linked to a man wielding absolute power who, though physically worn out, was mentally indefatigable. Hitler reeled out orders to which nobody any longer paid attention, except for the few faithful who were waiting with him in the bunker for their last hour. 'We are bound to the stake,' someone remarked to me. 'The flames all around us haven't yet reached our island, but the deadly embers are already burning us.'

During the first few days of the capital's encirclement, the question of the military command of Berlin illustrated the confusion that reigned in the minds of those in the bunker. General Helmuth Reymann had initially been appointed but he was not really suitable, so a replacement was quickly sought. Hitler insisted that he be chosen not necessarily for experience or rank, but for his fanaticism and faith in victory. Burgdorf, chief of the Army personnel department, proposed the appointment of a lieutenant colonel of the Grossdeutschland Division, about thirty years old, holder of the Knight's Cross with Oak-Leaves, whose 'faith' he totally guaranteed. Hitler had immediately given his agreement. The key formula of *fanatisch gläubig* (fanatical belief) was enough for him. Promptly promoted to general, this young officer had been given full powers to command all the units deployed in Berlin. By good fortune, however, both for him and for the defenders of the capital, he had been wounded and sent to hospital, so was no longer available.

Once this absurd solution had proved unrealisable, Hitler and Burgdorf agreed to target the name of Colonel Ernst Kaether, chief of staff of the Army *Nationalsozialistische Führungsoffiziere* (NFSO). His sole qualification for the post was his reputation as a good Nazi and his Knight's Cross. Several hours were sufficient to evaluate the capacities of this man to fulfil his arduous mission, and to cancel his appointment. Now Hitler turned to General Helmuth Weidling, commander of the LVI Panzer Corps, attached to the Ninth Army fighting to the southeast of Berlin. There was no news of him for three days; then, on the morning of 23 April, the general called the bunker to make his report. Krebs duly informed him that he had been condemned to death for desertion. That same afternoon, the general showed up at the bunker to protest his innocence. Impressed by him, Hitler did an about-turn and decided that the man whom he had intended to execute for cowardice in face of the enemy was now needed to conduct the defence of Berlin...

SINCE 23 APRIL, the bombardment of the city had been incessant. In the bunker, shaken at regular intervals by the artillery fire pounding the ministries' quarter, nerves became more and more frayed. Above our heads Berlin was burning, yet we knew nothing of what was actually going on behind the heavy thumps of explosions that came ever closer, the shuddering of the concrete walls and the dust falling from the ceilings. You only had to stand at any of the bunker exits and sniff the air to sense, amid the fire and smoke, that death was prowling. Fear was no longer disguised. In the passages, everyone talked about the situation, explored all the possibilities and debated what was best to do when the Russians eventually appeared at the bunker entrance. Suicide seemed one obvious way out. Hitler had declared on several occasions that he did not wish to survive defeat. Each of us faced the question of his own death and tried to tackle it in stark detail. It had become the number one subject of conversation in the bunker. Should one resort to the pistol or swallow a phial of prussic acid? If the former, which would be better: a bullet in the jaw or in the head?

In this tense atmosphere, discipline was relaxed. The rules that until now had been strictly observed were no longer followed. On the upper floor cigarettes were smoked in the passages and anterooms. The cellars of the Chancellery contained generous reserve stocks of wine and schnaps. Security guards, secretaries and employees arranged small parties upstairs, in the corridor which served as the dining room. Bottles were scattered everywhere. On the top floor, Krebs, Burgdorf and Bormann had formed a triumvirate of drinkers, drowning their anxiety day by day in alcohol. Krebs, like the others, didn't have much to do and depended entirely on the few scraps of information that I was able to furnish him. Bormann could only rely upon what reached him through Party channels. Ultimately, the trio made no further use of the rooms of the *Vorbunker* and spent the night huddled up in armchairs in the passage leading to the Führer's apartments. Krebs and Burgdorf had been friends since the time of the Reichswehr. In Army circles they had a reputation for being fond of their booze. In the course of one of their evening drinking sessions, General Wilhelm Burgdorf, principal adjutant to Hitler and head of the Army personnel department, had blamed Bormann, head of the Party Chancellery and secretary to Hitler, and through him the Nazi leaders. This dedicated National Socialist had accused them of having got fat on the backs of the German people, recognising that he had made a serious mistake. Krebs had been forced to mediate so that the inseparable clique could continue their terminal drinking sessions.

From necessity as much as from conviction, Boldt and I distanced ourselves from all this disorder. Our work helped us to keep clear heads in the hysterical atmosphere of this 'house of fools'. We shared a room, beds one above the other, two desks and two telephones, along the corridor that crossed the *Vorbunker* situated in the New Chancellery. General Krebs had a

bed in the same room. The occupants of the bunker quickly
came to realise that I was responsible for gathering military
information for Krebs and Hitler. I prudently kept away from
this rabble, for fear of saying too much and running the risk of
being denounced. Suddenly, Boldt and I had become important,
almost indispensable. Worn out by worry and waiting, the
recluses of the bunker had nothing else to do but shuffle up and
down the corridors, on the look-out for information. Whenever
we appeared, they crowded round us, asking what was new.
Although we were only junior officers, our value was incalcu-
lable. All of a sudden, it seemed opportune not to ignore the
military personnel, but to be agreeable and even make promises
to them.

IN THOSE FINAL days, Ambassador Walter Hewel, Ribbentrop's liaison officer, was one of the people who came to
question me. He was a realist with whom I could talk quite
freely, one of the rare 'old soldiers' who knew the world and
looked on Hitler, at the end, with a highly critical eye. Even
Bormann, who had never paid me the least attention, became
friendly. On the night of 27–28 April, towards midnight, he
went so far as to show me recognition. Boldt and I were in our
office, busy phoning and updating our maps, when Bormann
knocked on the door. 'I shall never forget the way in which you
are working so conscientiously so late at night,' remarked the
Brown Eminence, somewhat the worse for drink. 'If we get out

of here alive, I promise you I'll see to it personally that each of you receives a nobiliary estate.' Boldt and I just looked at each other in silence. We really didn't have time for that. Meanwhile Bormann tipsily staggered out...

Torn between survival and suicide, the inhabitants of the bunker teetered from hope to resignation. In this desperate state of chaos, Hitler wandered with dragging step, white as a sheet, arm trembling, sick and exhausted. He, like the others, had nothing to do but await an improbable reversal of events. He had neither briefings, nor meetings, nor decisions to take. Apathetic or hysterical by turns, he emerged from his private apartments to chat with someone or other, roaming the corridors in search of the faintest sign of hope. Was the end truly inevitable or could the great revolution prophesied by Goebbels still come to pass?

SOMEONE WHO HAD until then remained in the background of Hitler's immediate entourage now came increasingly to the fore. Eva Braun usually resided in Bavaria. At the beginning of March, when the danger of Berlin being encircled became evident, she had taken the train back to the capital, against Hitler's wishes, and at the end of April took her place among the community of idlers in the bunker. I often came across her in the corridor, in front of his apartments, deep in conversation with one of the Führer's secretaries, or sometimes with Magda Goebbels. Of medium height, with a good figure, slim and

Eva Braun

photograph: Getty Images

blonde, Eva Braun looked less than her thirty years, thanks to cleverly applied make-up. Always well dressed, her furs aroused envy. In short, she had chic. Those who knew her better than I did, because they joined her for the evening tea session, said that intellectually she had little else to offer than occasional chitchat on art or the theatre, her original profession. I don't know why Hitler was attracted to Eva Braun; he was an ordinary-looking, shabbily dressed individual in the shadow of this elegant woman. The contrast between the two of them was striking.

LINKS WITH THE outside world were not yet completely cut. A few aircraft were still parked at Gatow airport. On 23 April, after Keitel and Jodl, Hitler had received a visit from Speer, come to bid him farewell. At the time, I didn't understand what the Minister of Armaments expected of Hitler. His mission must have ended in failure but doubtless he wished to greet his mentor for the last time. In the afternoon, Hitler received a telegram from Göring which set the powder alight. The Reichsmarschall requested that he be entrusted to take over direction of the Reich, in keeping with what had been arranged should the Führer be isolated, taken captive or rendered incapable of giving orders:

'Mein Führer! In view of your decision to remain at your post in the fortress of Berlin, I now ask you, in conformity with your decree of 29 June 1941, in which you appointed me your deputy,

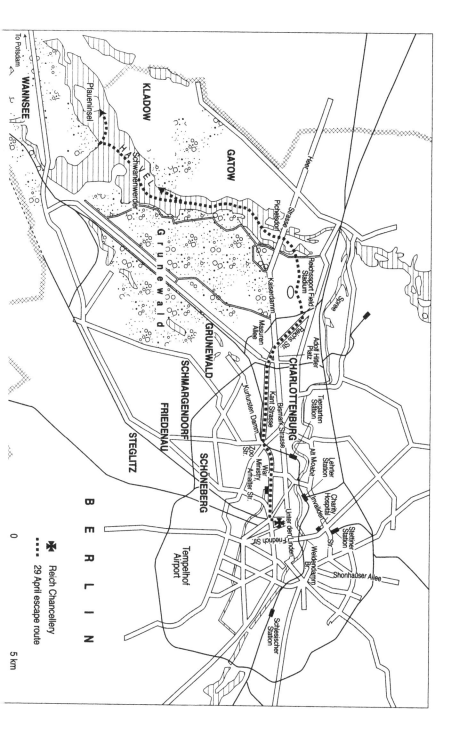

to hand over to me immediately full powers within the Reich. If no reply reaches me by ten o'clock tonight, I shall assume that you have lost your freedom of action and that the conditions laid down in your decree have been fulfilled, and I shall act in the best interests of our country and our people. No words can express what I feel for you in these, the most difficult, hours of my life. May God protect you. Your loyal Hermann Göring.'

A second telegram from Göring, inviting Ribbentrop for a consultation, finally convinced Hitler that this smacked of 'shameful treachery'. After a terrifying outburst, Hitler stripped Göring of all his titles and functions. By order of Bormann, Göring was at once taken prisoner by a detachment of SS.

APPOINTED COMMANDER-IN-CHIEF of the Luftwaffe, General Robert Ritter von Greim, a crony of Hitler's and with little ability, received the order to present himself at the double to the Führer. I found it absolutely crazy for the new head of the Air Force to run such a risk, simply for the pleasure of receiving the halo of loyalty from Hitler. Yet this obedient soldier, without pausing a second, had set off from Munich, together with his companion, Hanna Reitsch, the famous test pilot of the Luftwaffe. Arriving at Gatow airport in western Berlin, Greim and Reitsch then boarded a Fieseler-Storch. Over the Grunewald forest, the plane took a hit from a Soviet anti-aircraft gun and Greim was wounded in the foot. Hanna Reitsch managed to seize the controls and land the aircraft near the

Joachim von Ribbentrop

photograph: akg-images

Brandenburg Gate. Taken immediately on a stretcher to the bunker, Greim was treated by Hitler's last remaining surgeon, SS-Standartenführer Dr Ludwig Stumpfegger. Far from being disheartened by his unfortunate experience, Greim said that in the course of his subsequent meetings with Hitler he had discovered a 'fount of youth'.

THE RUSSIANS WERE closing in on the city centre. There was fighting on the Alexanderplatz. Tempelhof airport had fallen. While Soviet artillery rained tons of rockets and bombs on Berlin, its defenders, deprived of air support, were running acutely short of munitions. North of the capital, the Third Panzer Army was attacked on 25 April, south of Stettin, by the Army Group of Marshal Rokossovsky. Their remnants retreated westward without encountering any opposition. Outside Berlin, the Soviets rapidly gained ground in Pomerania and Mecklenburg. By order of Hitler, the Ninth Army remained on the banks of the Oder. All calls from General Busse asking for authorisation to withdraw towards Berlin had been ignored. On 27 April, far too late, the Ninth Army received the totally illusory order to attack in a westward direction, with the aim of linking up with Wenck's Army. Many soldiers died in the forests to the south of Berlin or were taken prisoner.

For all that, the death-throes were not yet over. In the hectic atmosphere of the bunker, hope was revived as the time came for using up the last reserves. Since the start, Hitler had pinned his hopes on the army of General Wenck. Young, dynamic and competent, Wenck could still call on troops consisting of the last recruits from the Hitler Youth, ready to die on the battle-field. This was perhaps the last chance of changing the course of fate. But a clear-sighted observer could not be fooled. The difference between Wenck's forces – at best several divisions – and the two Russian Army Groups with dozens of infantry and tank divisions, was all too conspicuous. However great the courage of the soldiers or the command qualities of the officers, it was impossible to expect miracles. Given the size of the enemy forces, it was astonishing that the battle even occurred. After reassembling in southern Brandenburg, Wenck's army went on the offensive south of Potsdam.

On 27 April, towards midday, I had the OKW on the telephone. Wenck had reached Ferch, a village some dozen kilometres from Potsdam and twenty kilometres south-west of Berlin. I knew that the commander of the Twelfth Army had only three divisions in proper working order, and no tanks or fighters, but this unexpected information struck me like an electric shock. I immediately charted Wenck's advance on my map and rushed into the bunker. Krebs and Hitler were in the Führer's office. 'I bring you some good news,' I announced, spreading out the map on the table. 'Wenck has reached Ferch.' While I was speaking, Hitler, spectacles on his nose, grabbed the map with trembling hands, his eyes bright and feverish, before turning to Krebs with a triumphant air, as if to say to him: 'I always told you so. We're getting there!' Above him, Krebs, his expression bland and impenetrable, adjusted his monocle and coldly replied: '*Mein Führer*, Ferch isn't Berlin!'

The news spread like wildfire. The occupants of the bunker, most of them lacking any military experience, once more regained their faith in Hitler's lucky star. Again I saw happy looks on faces as they asked me if the news about Wenck was really true. But the euphoria did not last long. Without news of Wenck for several more hours, we heard the same message of success on German radio: 'In their attack to liberate Berlin, the young divisions of Wenck's Army have reached the region south of Ferch.' In the bunker, a few had soon begun crying treason. If the Russians had not guessed it already, Wenck's objective seemed obvious. Next day, in communication with the OKW, we learned that Wenck's divisions had been forced to retreat towards the west. By evening, the intelligence left no doubt that the attack had failed. The last illusions drifted away. With all hope now definitely gone, everyone became preoccupied once more with death. Hitler had made known his intention of putting an end to his life. Rumour had it that he would fire a bullet through his head and that Eva Braun would take poison. 'It's just like a morgue here!' exclaimed someone, voicing the general feeling.

Yet in spite of the uncertainty, with backs to the wall, the impulse to survive was too strong. Mad projects continued to be discussed. On the evening of 26 April, General Weidling, military commander of Berlin, had suggested an evacuation of Hitler and all the bunker residents during the night of 28 April. An escort of tanks and soldiers would effect a breakthrough to the west and link up with the remaining Army Group Vistula. Hitler had rejected all such pleas. In truth, everyone was resigned to the inevitable. The Soviet forces were only a few hundred metres from the Chancellery. They had captured the station and bridge at Potsdam. The Potsdamer Platz was under sustained fire from their machine guns. If the SS Mohnke brigade, supposedly protecting the Reich Chancellery with 2,000 men, put up no resistance, the Soviet troops would be at the gates of the bunker within a few minutes.

DURING THE NIGHT of 27–28 April, the bombardments redoubled in intensity. In the concrete block of the *Führerbunker* we felt the vibrations of the uninterrupted thunder of Russian artillery as it pounded the Chancellery. The ceiling of the *Vorbunker*, much less thick, was in danger of collapsing under the shelling. Water trickled into all parts of the *Kannenberggang*, through the gaps torn out by rockets. The emergency lighting, powered by a generator, flickered on and off, often throwing the bunker into darkness and disarray. Filth piled up everywhere. Waste matter was no longer removed. Mattresses were stacked together higgledy-piggledy in the corridors. Dust and smoke filtered in through the openings and ventilators.

On the evening of 28 April, Heinz Lorenz brought in a message of considerable importance. A dispatch from Reuters confirmed the news broadcast that morning by Radio Stockholm and conveyed to Hitler around midday. Reichsführer SS Heinrich Himmler had offered to surrender to the western Allies, who had rejected the proposal. Reuters reported that Himmler had let it be known that he could arrange an unconditional surrender that would be honoured. The Reichsführer regarded himself de facto as head of state, usurping Hitler's powers. This, to the Führer, was the mother of all treasons. The 'most faithful of the faithful' had made contact with the enemy – a step that not even Göring had dared take. 'Faithful Heinrich', whose SS carried the motto, 'Loyalty is my honour', had delivered him the ultimate stab in the back. Hitler gave vent to his fury and frustration for the final time.

THE DEFEAT OF Wenck's Army had sounded the death knell for all military hope. Now Himmler's treachery signalled the end of the regime. Division split the ranks from top to bottom. On the morning of 29 April, Krebs described to me the profound disillusionment of the Führer. After the failure of all his efforts, Hitler had positively decided to end his life. The little time that the Russians had left him might possibly be used to settle the question of the succession. To the surprise of all the bunker inhabitants, he had also decided to wed Eva Braun. In fact, they had been married during the night by a civilian officer from the Ministry of Propaganda, in Party uniform with the *Volk-sturm* insignia, and with Goebbels and Bormann as witnesses. Krebs had joined the guests in an improvised wedding meal. The air was heavy. No one was in the mood for rejoicing. Death was already lurking in the wake of this doomed couple. While the wedding guests were still assembled, Hitler retired to dictate to his secretary, Traudl Junge, his political and personal wills. To general astonishment, he did not choose as his successor one of the Party chiefs, such as Goebbels or Bormann, but instead Grand Admiral Dönitz. The commander-in-chief of the Navy was a dedicated Nazi, but nobody expected that the Führer, at the point of death, would place his trust in a military man.

One man was missing from the wedding table – Hitler's brother-in-law, Hermann Fegelein. Obsessed by the criminal activities of his entourage, Hitler had noticed his non-appearance and sent to look for him. Several hours before his arrest, Fegelein had called me from his apartment to get the latest news on the military situation. This inveterate careerist had no desire to end his days with Hitler. For some time he had sought the means to make his escape. SS-Sturmbannführer Högl found him in his Charlottenburg apartment and led him away under escort with a detachment of the SD. Immediately dismissed and stripped of his titles, Fegelein was locked in a prison cell. The announcement of Himmler's treachery proved fatal to him. Hitler accused him of being in collusion with Himmler. An

Karl Dönitz

photograph: Time & Life Pictures/Getty Images

improvised SS tribunal condemned him to death for complicity in treason. On the night of 28–29 April, I had seen him pass by my open door in the corridor, accompanied by four SS men, dishevelled in appearance, epaulettes and decorations torn from his uniform. Fegelein was shot at dawn in the Chancellery garden. Hitler had ended his wedding night by taking revenge on his brother-in-law.

NOT ALL THOSE who were still inside the 'morgue' of the bunker were called upon to die. Greim and Reitsch achieved the impossible by taking off from the Brandenburg Gate and landing safely at Rechlin airport. Early in the morning, after Krebs had told me about the events of the previous night, I put him in touch by phone with Jodl at Wehrmacht headquarters. Jodl informed him that the front had collapsed everywhere; then communications were cut when the captive balloon over Rheinberg was shot down by the Russians. The same day, the OKW had to flee before the advancing Soviet forces.

That, for me, was the signal for departure. I decided to go to see Krebs and tell him bluntly that I had no intention of getting myself killed in the bunker. I had reached the limit I had set myself. My job had been to collect as much intelligence as possible and transfer it to the maps. The interruption of the last link with the OKW meant that I could no longer do my work. My military duty was over and all I had to do was look after my own welfare. It was a personal decision, arrived at after much

thought without talking to anyone; a hard decision and potentially fraught with consequences. I risked being taken for a
deserter, which would mean immediate execution. By virtue
of a decree by Goebbels, Reich commissar for Berlin, any man
still capable of carrying arms was forbidden to leave the capital
without authorisation. SS commandos or military police were
arresting German soldiers suspected of desertion. If they were
unable to show a permit, they faced a brutal death. But I felt an
utter stranger in this underground world and had no wish, above
all, to die like a rat. I had to take the initiative. One day more
and I might not be able to reach the river Havel and cross the
Russian lines.

Since my arrival in the bunker I had several times been asked
what was the best way to get out of Berlin. Because of my
involvement with maps, I was quite familiar with the situation
above ground. I had discovered two itineraries. The first lay
through the Grunewald forest, the second by boat down the
river Havel to the Wannsee. German troops still held the central
part of the ministries' quarter, the 'zoo', a narrow corridor
running from the Zoo station westward to reach the Havel, as
well as a few scattered strongpoints.

Around 9.00 p.m., after telling Boldt, I went to find my boss
to ask for his authorisation to leave the bunker. I did not then
know that three messengers – SS-Standartenführer Wilhelm
Zander, Bormann's aide-de-camp, Major Willi Johannmeier,
Hitler's Army adjutant, and Heinz Lorenz, acting press officer –

had already departed that morning to hand over copies of the Führer's will to Dönitz, Schörner and Party national head-quarters (NSDAP) in Munich. I asked Krebs to authorise us to go and fight alongside the troops in Berlin or endeavour to join Wenck. The general hesitated and then answered that he was uncertain how Hitler would react to my proposal. We had a good working relationship, he liked having me around to do the donkey work, and he was a bit sorry, no doubt, to have to give it up. Krebs added that he could not take such a decision alone and that he would need to speak to General Burgdorf, Hitler's principal adjutant and chief of the Army personnel department.

Burgdorf was all in favour of the idea and took the opportunity to authorise his own aide-de-camp, Lieutenant Colonel Weiss, to come along with me. In the morning, after a meeting with Hitler, Burgdorf passed on to him my request. The Führer was now determined to end his life, which was only a matter of time. He was quite indifferent to the fate of three young officers and he raised no objection. We awaited the decision in our room. Burgdorf came to announce it and requested us to take formal leave of Hitler.

Around 1.00 p.m. on the afternoon of 29 April, Lieutenant Colonel Weisse, Captain Boldt and I went to see him in his office. Since I had initiated the scheme, I did the talking. To my great astonishment, after all the dramatic happenings of the night, Hitler seemed very calm and relaxed. I explained our plan to him, with the two options. The first, to go through the Grunewald forest, seemed the more risky because the front was very fragmented in that sector. The second, to row down the Havel by canoe, assumed that we could count on two kilometres of open water at Spandau, plus the presence of German troops between Pichelsdorf and Berlin. Hitler immediately picked this route as being the better. Ever a maniac for detail, he advised us to look for a boat with an electric motor to avoid making any noise and attracting the attention of Russian troops. I thought this unrealistic because a larger boat would immediately be spotted. My idea was to choose as small a boat as possible, a flexible Klepper fabric dinghy, very low in the water and thus less conspicuous. But to conduct a technical discussion here and now on the ideal type of vessel to choose risked capsizing the entire venture. I agreed with him, therefore, that his idea made a lot of sense and that we would fall back on something else in case of absolute necessity. Hitler gave us the official mission order to join Wenck's Army, and asked us to convey his greetings to him. He got up, shook hands with us and wished us good luck. The conversation had lasted twenty minutes. In his expression, I believe I detected a suspicion of envy. Here were three men, young and healthy, who had the chance to save their skin – something that he no longer had.

IT WAS MY last conversation with Hitler. Twenty-four hours later, he was dead. At the very same moment, we were under fire from Russian artillery at Pichelsdorf, with units of the Hitler Youth for company. We were not confident of coming out alive from this chaos, but we were happy at last to have freedom of action. Behind us, there was only death. Before us opened the opportunity of life.

ELEVEN

Return to life

Amid the storm of gun and rifle fire, we walked all the way down Hermann-Göring Strasse towards Tiergarten. A few minutes earlier, Rudolf Weiss, Gerhard Boldt and I had hastily donned helmets, snatched a sub-machine gun and bullets, and brought along a few provisions and maps. To prevent being too easily spotted, I had cut the two red bands – the distinctive insignia of a general staff officer – off my trousers. The Soviet troops were no more than 800 metres from the Chancellery. We had moved on for some four hours among trees cut to ribbons, leaping over shell craters and doing our best to avoid the gunfire. When we reached the Zoo, we took shelter for a while in the planetarium. There, looking up at the dome of the building I saw it sprinkled with stars, but there was a huge gap in the middle through which there was a view of the real sky!

Near the Zoo station, at the south-west corner of Tiergarten, hundreds of people were crammed into a shelter where it was almost impossible to breathe, surmounted by an anti-aircraft tower. Early in the evening, we had crossed Charlottenburg to Halensee, to the west of the Kurfürstendamm. Night was falling and we had no idea how to get to the river Havel. A lieutenant colonel from the Berlin defence force, responsible for that sector, put an armoured car at our disposal, with a guide who took us across Charlottenburg to the Olympic stadium.

At dawn on 30 April, we resumed our progress along the Heerstrasse, in the direction of Pichelsdorf on the Havel. It was light enough for us to distinguish three Russian tanks, their guns pointed towards the bridge. The soldiers did not react when we crossed, doubtless because they were asleep. On the other side, the Hitler Youth in position with their rocket-launchers had not budged. Throughout the day, we searched for a boat from one of the various nautical clubs located on the Pichelsdorf peninsula, awaiting nightfall – fortunately one without a moon – to paddle downriver in a canoe as far as the reed beds of the Pfauen Insel (Peacock Island). Gliding silently along the bank, we heard the conversations of the Russian soldiers occupying the villas. On 1 May, at dawn, we landed on the island. 'Halt, who goes there?' shouted someone in German, demanding our identification password. We were much relieved that they had not opened fire on us...

THIS LAST REMNANT of German troops was planning to cross the Wannsee on the night of 1–2 May to join up with what was left of Wenck's army south of Potsdam. We had no alternative but to follow them. Surrounded by gunfire, we had to surmount an anti-tank obstacle before making our escape by plunging into the pine forest. At one crossroad, Weiss suggested going off to reconnoitre and see what was going on. We followed him at a distance but he did not return, and we assumed he had been captured. Boldt and I then passed the entire day of 2 May hiding in a ditch, while the Russians rummaged through the woods with dogs. All of a sudden I saw Boldt turn and swallow in a single gulp the tube of pills that a German military doctor had given him the previous night. This act took me by complete surprise. Boldt was a brave man who had been decorated with the Iron Cross for having destroyed five Russian tanks with a grenade. Shocked by his action, I really went for him. Fortunately we had eaten hardly anything for twenty-four hours; his stomach could not sustain such a massive dose of sleeping tablets and he spewed up the whole lot.

We had now thrown caution to the winds. I was afraid that the Russians, who were not more than a hundred metres away, would eventually discover us. When night fell, I carried Boldt, in his weakened state, across my shoulders along the Wannsee. We were reluctant to squat in an empty house because we knew that the Soviets took advantage of darkness to carry out their looting and raping. I noticed an allotment of railway workers' kitchen gardens, the kind of place that would not interest the enemy, and settled Boldt down on a bed inside one of the huts. Among the items stored there was a large sack full of porridge oats. I heated some up in a saucepan and, famished, we devoured our meal. We stayed there for two nights, until 3 May. Meanwhile, we swapped our uniforms for some workers' old clothes which made us look like absolute scarecrows. The only thing we didn't manage to find was footwear; so we had to hang on to our officers' boots, concealing them under our trousers. Streams of foreign workers wearing a white armband had taken to the roads in flight. My idea was to pass ourselves off as workmen from Luxembourg. Should we meet any Russian soldiers, we would pretend to be speaking French.

The trick was only partly successful. Several times we almost got arrested. We had decided to spend the night at the former German training camp of Jüterbog. At the bridge over the Teltow canal, we ran into columns of Russian soldiers making their way westward along both lanes of the motorway, accompanied by trucks crammed with furniture and other articles looted from the surrounding neighbourhood. We were about to cross the bridge when an officer of the Soviet secret police, identifiable from his green braid, asked me in shaky German the way to Jüterbog. 'Don't understand,' I mumbled in French, 'I'm from Luxembourg.' At that very moment, in a flash, I caught a glimpse of Lieutenant Colonel Weiss, sitting in a truck full of German prisoners. Weiss did not recognise me, I gave nothing away and the Russian officer drove off in his vehicle. Weiss was to spend five years in a prisoner-of-war camp in Poland.

LATER, WE SPENT the night in a bathing hut on the shores of a lake, near Trebbin. We were fast asleep, confident we were safe, when a Russian patrol woke us up, shining their torches on us. I had got rid of my pistol some time beforehand and we had no compromising objects with us. When they made us if to search us, I realised that the bullets from my revolver had slipped into the lining of my jacket. Thank God, the Soviets were completely taken in.

In an abandoned village, we watched the arrival of a truck filled with troops dressed in the green uniforms of military units of the Soviet secret police (NKVD); they surrounded us, not wholly convinced of our Luxembourg identity. When their leader flung me, flat on my stomach, face down, into a ditch, I was sure my last hour had come. This time, the 'bolshies' were bound to kill or arrest us. The Russian, however, was only interested in my officer's boots. It was 8 May, the day of the German surrender. In their victory euphoria, the Soviet soldiers let us go free. We got away as quickly as we could, running in our socks to the nearest village where someone provided me with some slippers before I unearthed an old pair of cloth shoes.

The following day, not far from Wittenberg, we again ran into a Russian checkpoint. We had been directed, together with other displaced persons, to a foreign workers' camp. We had walked a couple of kilometres to a farm where we registered as workmen from Luxembourg, under false identities. Someone came to see us and began to talk in the Luxembourg dialect, and we tried to explain that we had been away from home for a long time. Without replying, he moved off, shrugging his shoulders. We lost no time getting out of the place, continuing our journey towards Wittenberg. Numerous survivors of the Ninth Army were pouring across the Oder in the direction of the Elbe, trying to join General Wenck's Twelfth Army. They trudged through woods to avoid being sighted by the Russians. At Wittenberg, we took some time to cross the Elbe. The bridge had been damaged and we were threatened by a Russian soldier: *'Niet! Niet! Deutsche Soldaten!'* Luckily, we managed to find a fisherman to take us across.

THE FINAL OBSTACLE to cross was the Mulde, near Dessau, which marked the frontier with the American zone. The river was some 80 metres wide and the water was extremely cold. We had been warned that, from the other bank, the Americans were firing on anything that moved. On 11 May, we swam across the river without trouble, relieved and delighted to have reached our goal. The next day we separated: Boldt headed north for Lübeck and I continued towards Leipzig to join my wife and son who lived about twenty kilometres from the city. I travelled the last bit of the motorway by bicycle, winding my way through columns of American soldiers. At Leipzig, on 12 May, near the

Völkerschlachtdenkmal, the monument to the Battle of the Nations (Leipzig), commemorating the victory against the armies of Napoleon, a big American soldier stopped me and refused to believe my Luxembourg worker's tale. Relieved of the 2,000 marks and my watch, which the Russians had left me, I spent a couple of days in a cellar with other prisoners before being transported by truck to the Helfta camp. So, at the end of almost five years of war, I now found myself behind barbed wire, together with 25,000 German soldiers, with a tin of petits pois each day for five people.

I was deeply disappointed not to have been able to rejoin my family, but the essential thing for me was to have escaped the clutches of the Russians for a third time; first, at Stalingrad in January 1943 and then, six months later, in the Taganrog region. I was convinced that I would be treated as a prisoner-of-war by the western Allies, in keeping with the Geneva Convention, and quickly set free. I had never committed any acts contrary to the rules of war and I had a clear conscience. In short, the war was over.

IN THE HELFTA camp near Eisleben in Saxe-Anhalt, I met an old friend whom I had known during the war, a German diplomat who spoke fluent English and acted as interpreter. He advised me to reveal my true identity, and I did exactly that when I was officially registered as a prisoner-of-war on 15 May 1945. In due course the zone was evacuated by the Americans and taken over by the British. Staff officers were taken to another camp at Eselheide, not far from Paderborn in North Rhine-Westphalia. From there we were transferred to a camp in Belgium, in the neighbourhood of Ostend. There were about sixty of us, several generals, including General Wenck, and staff officers. It was during this period, as a result of information provided by the British, that I began to become aware of the true nature and extent of the Nazi extermination system. I was deeply shocked. I could not believe, as a Christian, the terrible things that Germans had been doing.

BEFORE CHRISTMAS, I was told that I was to be taken by plane, escorted by a British major, to an interrogation camp at Bad Nenndorf, near Hanover. This did not augur well. Before going aboard, the officer loaded his gun in front of me, remarking: 'Bullets are cheap!' We landed near a building that had formerly been a public baths. The baths had been removed and the bathing huts transformed into cells. Inside were two bunk beds, a table and two stools, but no washing or toilet facilities. In Belgium they had given me a uniform which I had to return before leaving. This time I had to wear prison garb. I protested in vain, demanding to be treated as an officer, in accordance with international convention.

After spending twenty-fours alone in my cell, with very little food, I was joined the next day by a little bald man, about fifty years old with a ruddy face, dressed in the same prisoner's uniform, cut off at the knee. It was none other than General Kurt Zeitzler, Guderian's predecessor. The way in which the British were treating a senior officer shocked me. Zeitzler was happy to see me because, unlike him, I spoke English, which could prove useful with the somewhat uncivilised guards. I had only met him once, when I had arrived at the operations department of general headquarters, at the beginning of April 1944. During the four weeks of captivity that we spent together, Zeitzler held forth at great length on his experiences as head of the Army, particularly his arguments with Hitler concerning Stalingrad.

We had nothing to read. As we were both Protestants, I was told that if I asked my guards for a Bible, they could not refuse. So they brought us an enormous prayer book, no doubt belonging to a nearby church, which I proceeded to read aloud, page by page. Zeitzler liked playing cards and I devised a game with scraps of paper. When the interrogations began, we were herded into a bigger cell with eight other prisoners, all officers of the Abwehr. The remaining detainees comprised a mixture of SS criminals who had worked in the concentration camps, former managerial staff from large German companies and military intelligence officers. We were put to work cleaning the kitchens and pigsties, and carrying coal. General Zeitzler, also set to forced labour, had heart trouble. I later learned that he had been taken to hospital, cared for and quickly freed. I never saw him again: he died in 1963.

THE MAN EMPLOYED to interrogate me, Major Oughton, asked me very detailed questions for hours on end, in a cold, detached tone, but always with a purpose. Most of the time, our conversations had to do with the last days in the bunker. I discovered subsequently that Major Oughton was the assumed name of Hugh Trevor-Roper, a member of the British secret service and a future Oxford professor, author of an acclaimed book published shortly after the war.* I told him of events as I had experienced them, without any pressure on his part, and he soon understood that I had nothing to hide.

One day, I even had to call on him to get me out of a very unpleasant situation. Every evening, a highly aggressive guard came to check up on us in our cell. On one occasion I had a trifling argument with him and he put me in an isolation cell. For three days, from morning till evening, my guards forced me to scratch the paint on the tiles with my nails, and to rub and wash down the cell, which was already clean. They sprayed me with water while kicking me. At the end of the day they removed my wet clothing and left me to sleep naked on the damp floor. It was spring and very cold outside. I felt humiliated and abandoned. I had no news of my family at this time, and did not know where they were or even whether they were alive. I asked to see Major Oughton, saying that I had something important to tell him. My guards allowed me to dress and

---

*Hugh Redwald Trevor-Roper, *The Last Days of Hitler*, Macmillan 1947, Pan Books 2002. Trevor-Roper died 26 January 2003.

conducted me to him. I described the treatment that his coun-
trymen were making me endure and protested against such
abuse. Although he did not give anything away, my complaints
clearly embarrassed him, for he made me his excuses and everything returned to normal.

AT THE BEGINNING of summer 1946, I was once again transferred by car, handcuffs on my wrists, to the camp near Ostend
and then, in the autumn, to Munsterlager, a former German
training establishment in the Lüneberg Heide region, south of
Hamburg, where I remained until late summer 1947. Some of
us were then set free. My interrogations were over but the British
were even more wary than the Americans. They feared especially that the *Werwolf* (werewolf) organisation founded by
Bormann and the Nazi Party during the final months of the war
might trigger off clandestine resistance to the occupying forces.
I presume that they kept me under guard for safety reasons,
either because I had been sent on missions by Hitler or his
entourage, or in order to compare my statements with those of
other prisoners. My proximity to Hitler during the last nine
months of the war rendered me more of a suspect than anyone
else. At the time I did not understand that this could be the
reason for detaining me longer. I had never been a member of
the Führer's close circle, but my presence in the bunker during
those last days complicated my case. The British found it
difficult to believe I was not a Nazi.

WITH SEVERAL OTHER comrades, including Colonel von Humboldt, a former member of the OKH, I was yet again taken to another camp at Adelheide, near Olenburg, in Niedersachsen, between Bremen and the North Sea, until my release in January 1948. It was a relatively modern barracks complex, built in 1938, with central heating. The buildings were linked by underground ducts which our British guardians had never examined closely. These huge pipes, connected to ventilation shafts, ran under the barbed wire fences. During the night, we crept 300 metres through them on hands and knees. I can still see General Hans Kreysing, an elderly general with asthma, crawling along the piping, preceded by his son-in-law, Major Schlegtendahl, an air pump in his hand to allow him to breathe. For several months, we were able in this way to see our families who brought us food, and to get out mail. The British never detected this mass-movement of moles. Nevertheless, not one of us tried to escape. If anyone had missed roll-call, the entire scheme would have been discovered. We were content to await our liberation; and indeed, after two and a half years of captivity I was finally set free to be rejoined with my family.

TWELVE

Sixty years later

Sixty years after these events, I still remind myself how very lucky I was to escape from the bunker and come out of that war alive. A host of guardian angels were watching over me. But my prayers were supplemented by the determination to survive. I still wake up at night thinking of episodes that could have had a fatal ending, key moments that hinged on a throw of the dice. That evening, for example, in the Stalingrad pocket, where I went on for longer than usual talking with my officers in the little earth bunker that served as my office. Ten metres away, a bomb had blown up the bunker where I normally slept... I always managed, at any rate, to escape the clutches of the Russians.

Richard von Weizsäcker was perhaps exaggerating when, in his speech to the Bundestag, on the fortieth anniversary of the German surrender, he described 8 May 1945 as 'the day of liberation'. It is true, of course, that on that day Germany finally rid itself of the 'brown plague'. At the same time, we felt we were on the brink of a precipice, about to tumble into chaos. The country was divided into four zones. Millions of people were worrying about their future. On 8 May I experienced more of a feeling of urgency and existentialist anguish than of liberation. As a soldier, I had the disagreeable impression of having been used as fodder for the adventures of a charlatan. I felt guilty for having served a criminal regime while remaining loyal to my convictions and my military obligations. Hitler had dragged us towards the abyss. As Helmut Schmidt, also a former Wehrmacht officer, remarked, I could not do otherwise than fight for Germany, but I never fought for Hitler. We had no desire for the war against Poland and did not understand that Hitler's intention was to attack the Soviet Union.

DURING MY CAPTIVITY, I had followed the progress of the Nuremberg trials and the death sentences pronounced against Keitel and Jodl in the autumn of 1946. Criminals who had brought Germany so low deserved to be punished, although I considered the condemnation of Jodl to be too harsh. A very sensitive question at that time was to ascertain whether the German Army itself was to be judged a criminal organisation and whether the staff officers would be found guilty en bloc. Stalin was demanding the elimination of 50,000 German officers. The Wehrmacht contained rather more than a thousand staff officers. Most of them were prisoners of the Allies, others were in Soviet hands. The Allies were thinking of sentencing them to forced labour in Germany, Madagascar or the Falkland Islands. The Nuremberg tribunal finally decided that we should not all be judged collectively. In December 1952, at the podium of the Bundestag, Konrad Adenauer assured all those who had borne arms and fought with honour of his 'esteem'. The Chancellor's remarks were not aimed at rehabilitating soldiers found guilty of crimes but of ending the isolation of those who felt that they alone bore the blame.

When I was freed, at the beginning of 1948, I started at rock bottom. In July 1945, with the assistance of the Swiss consul who had happened to take up residence on the estate of my parents-in-law, my wife and son had fled to the American zone. Several weeks later, the Russians had taken control of the Leipzig region, in agreement with the Allies. My wife had packed only what was absolutely necessary, leaving everything else behind. She had found lodgings at Tannhausen, a remote village in Bade-Wurtemberg, without any rail connection. When I rejoined them, all I had was my prisoner's uniform and an olive-green blanket from the US Army. Without a job or any professional qualification other than that of a soldier, I could not resume my law studies. I had to provide for the needs of my family. Friends helped me to find a livelihood with a publishing house in Munich.

LATER, I FOUND great satisfaction in my new functions in the service of the Bundeswehr. Friends involved in the process of German rearmament urged me to take part in the creation of a democratic military institution, under control of the civil authorities. Some of them, at the suggestion of Colonel von Bonin – an excellent soldier but a poor politician – argued in favour of a neutralised army, but most people, including myself, wanted to build up a new German army within an alliance, and supported integration with NATO.

A 'committee of approval' selected future officers so as to be certain that they had not been mixed up with National Socialism. I joined the FUS III (Führungsstab III), a department responsible for strategy and relations with NATO. It was a familiar area, and the people who worked with me had all maintained a critical attitude during the war. General Ulrich de Maizière, head of FUS III, had been adjutant to General von Trotha, successor to Bonin at the head of the operations department of the OKH. General Heusinger, my former boss at the operations department, was appointed chief of staff. In 1957, Hans Speidel took over command of the NATO land forces in Europe, to be replaced in 1963 by Kielmannsegg. In the early 1960s, Baudissin, with whom I had shared captivity for a few months, occupied several posts within NATO, at Fontainebleau and Paris.

After four years in Bonn, I represented Germany for three years at the Standing Group of NATO in Washington. I was the only German officer in the planning section of the Atlantic Alliance, led by three high-ranking officers, one American, one Englishman and one Frenchman. All the officers there had fought against Germany. I shared an office with one Danish and one Norwegian officer. The Dane had spent the entire war in the resistance and the Norwegian had fought against the Germans and escaped on a yacht to England. Both were aware that I had fought in Poland, France and on the Russian front; but the fact that I was a former officer of the Wehrmacht did not prevent us becoming friends. At that time, I also became friendly with Jacques Mitterand, an officer of the French Air Force and brother of the future President. Later, I was pleased to meet him at the bilateral staff meetings between France and Germany.

I AM NO PHILOSOPHER, but a realist. I have always tried to look on the past as objectively as possible, in the hope of increasing my knowledge rather than twisting a sword in the wound. The terrible experience of the war, the Nazi dictatorship and the Holocaust are all part of our history. A clear understanding of the past ought not to lead to a general and permanent sense of guilt for the generations to come, but it does carry the obligation of vigilance. Respect and protection for the dignity of human rights is written into our Constitution, and a democratic Germany, which has once more become a member and full partner of the international community, has a particular responsibility in this context. When history eventually clarifies memory, this has to be the best antidote to intolerance and the recurrence of delusions.

Glossary

Abwehr: Wehrmacht intelligence and counter-espionage service, headed by Admiral Canaris. In 1944 its foreign department was integrated with the central direction of Reich security.

Army: its effective strength might vary from 40,000 to 100,000 men.

Battalion: its composition and strength depended upon its function (infantry, tank, etc.).

Brigade: a formation between a regiment and a division in size.

Corps: an army corps comprised several divisions, usually from two to four.

Division: its numbers were very variable.

Gestapo (*Geheime Staatspolizei*): the state secret police, headed by SS-Gruppenführer Heinrich Müller.

Group: an army group was a collection of several armies under a single commander.

Kriegsakademie: school for staff officers, founded 15 October 1810 by Scharnhorst, shut down in accordance with the Versailles Treaty and reopened by Hitler in 1935.

NKVD: Soviet secret police controlled by Lavrenti Beria. Military units of the NKVD were attached to each command at the front.

OKH (*Oberkommando des Heeres*): In theory, the supreme command of the German Army; in practice, the operational command for the eastern front.

OKW (*Oberkommando der Wehrmacht*): Supreme command of the combined German armed forces, the Army, Luftwaffe and Kriegsmarine, controlled directly by Hitler through Field Marshal Keitel, chief of staff, and General Jodl, chief of the operations department. Operational command on all fronts except the eastern front.

Regiment: it comprised at least two or three battalions, potentially up to 2,000 men but often fewer.

RSHA: central office for Reich security, created in 1939, it grouped together the security police and the Party security service (SD, *Sicherheitdienst*, security service) and was headed by SS-Obergruppenführer Reinhard Heidrich, replaced after his assassination in Prague on 27 May 1942 by SS-Gruppenführer Ernst Kaltenbrunner.

Volksgerichtshof: people's court presided over by the Nazi judge Roland Freisler, set up to judge the conspirators of the failed plot of 20 July 1944.

Volkssturm: people's militia, created in 1944 by Heinrich Himmler to incorporate all able-bodied Germans aged from sixteen to sixty.

Ranks

BRITISH ARMY	WEHRMACHT	WAFFEN-SS
Private	Grenadier	SS Mann
Lance Corporal	Gefreiter	Sturmmann
Corporal	Obergefreiter	Rottenführer
Sergeant	Unteroffizier	Unterscharführer
Company Sergeant Major	Hauptfeldwebel	Hauptscharführer
Second Lieutenant	Leutnant	Untersturmführer
Lieutenant	Oberleutnant	Obersturmführer
Captain	Hauptmann	Hauptsturmführer
Major	Major	Sturmbannführer
Lieutenant Colonel	Oberstleutnant	Obersturmbannführer
Colonel/Brigadier	Oberst	Standartenführer
Brigadier General	Generalmajor	Brigadeführer
Major General	Generalleutnant	Gruppenführer
Lieutenant General	General der Infanterie	Obergruppenführer
General	Generaloberst	Oberstgruppenführer
Field Marshal	General Feldmarschall	Reichsführer SS

Index